DISCOVERING THE HUMAN MIND

DISCOVERING
THE HUMAN MIND
by Stuart Sutherland

Published by

in association with

The American Museum of Natural History

The author
Professor Stuart Sutherland is the Director of the Centre for
Research on Perception and Cognition at Sussex University,
England. This is one of the most important institutes for
psychological research in Europe. He is the author of about one
hundred scientific articles and a popular book about mental
breakdown that has been a bestseller around the world. In addition
to his teaching and research work, he often lectures in the United
States and contributes regularly to leading British newspapers.

The consultant
Dr Andrew Mathews, Professor of Psychology at St George's
Hospital Medical School, has had a distinguished career in both
research and teaching. He has been a research worker for the
Medical Research Council, a lecturer at the Institute of Psychiatry
of the University of London, and Senior Research Psychologist in
the Department of Psychiatry at Oxford before his appointment to
St George's in 1976. He has a long list of publications in the fields of
research and treatment and has published a major study of
agoraphobia.

The American Museum of Natural History
Stonehenge Press wishes to extend particular thanks to
Dr Thomas D. Nicholson, Director of the Museum, and Mr David
D. Ryus, Vice President, for their counsel and assistance in
creating this volume.

Stonehenge Press Inc.:
Publisher: John Canova
Editor: Ezra Bowen
Deputy Editor: Carolyn Tasker

Sceptre Books Ltd:
Editorial Consultant: James Clark
Managing Editor: Barbara Horn

Created, designed and produced by
Sceptre Books Ltd, London

Library of Congress Card Number: 81-52417
Printed in U.S.A. by Rand McNally & Co.
First printing

ISBN 0-86706-009-3
ISBN 0-86706-060-3 (lib. bdg.)
ISBN 0-86706-029-8 (retail ed.)

Set in Monophoto Rockwell Light by
SX Composing Ltd, Rayleigh, Essex, England
Separation by Scan Studios Ltd, Dublin, Ireland

Contents

The World of The Human Mind

The human mind is possibly the most familiar and the most mysterious entity in the known universe. It is familiar because we all have direct experience of our own minds. It is mysterious because we cannot see it or touch it, nor do we understand how mind relates to matter. Moreover, we are not conscious of much of what happens even in our own minds. Part of the task of psychology is to reveal these unconscious processes.

In ancient times, people tried to explain the behavior of all things by saying each contained a mind or was directed by a superior mind, a god. For example, winds were the breath of gods. As man came to see that matter obeys precise laws of its own, he learned how to manipulate it. Modern technology is the result of this long process of learning to control matter. More recently, man began to study the mind scientifically. There are two ways of doing this. The first is used by psychologists, who investigate what the mind produces – that is, people's behavior. They can also investigate patterns of personality, the mechanisms of memory or the factors that lie behind intelligence. They can carry out systematic observations to discover how and why mental disorders arise. From this kind of information they try to infer the mental processes that underlie behavior, most of which are unconscious.

A second way of studying the mind is to investigate the brain – the bodily organ that governs all mental activities. Neurophysiologists have worked out how nerve cells conduct information through the brain and how they switch the routing of messages at the points where they are connected. Neuroanatomists study how the brain is wired up. Neurologists and psychologists examine the ways in which the mind is affected when different parts of the brain are damaged. Neurochemists investigate the ways different drugs affect the brain and lead to changes in thought and behavior. Psychiatrists and clinical psychologists treat the mentally ill and also conduct research on the causes and treatment of mental illness. Investigating the mind in distress often throws light on different aspects of how the mind works normally.

The aim of all this study is to explain how the mind works. Which of its activities are people born with and which have to be learned? How does behavior develop throughout life? What underlies different aspects of behavior and where are the centers in the brain that control different mental functions? One should not forget that the mind has developed in the course of evolution and that its activities have survival value.

The study of the mind is at a particularly exciting stage at the moment. Since the first Laboratory of Psychology was founded in Germany in 1882 a vast number of psychological experiments have been carried out all over the world. Ingenious new methods of performing such experiments are constantly being devised. Brain scientists have discovered how to record the activity of a single nerve cell, using needle-like electrical probes called microelectrodes, whose tips are so small they are invisible to the naked eye. The electron microscope allows the neuroanatomist to look at the tiniest details of how a nerve cell functions. Through exceedingly thin tubes tiny electric pulses or minute amounts of chemicals can be delivered to a particular part of the brain.

When the information gathered by psychologists and other scientists is put together, it provides a scientific understanding of much of the mind's activities. For example, scientists have discovered a great deal about how our senses work, how language is controlled and understood, how basic drives such as hunger, thirst and sex are regulated, and how people solve problems or commit material to memory.

There are aspects of the mind on which less progress has been made, and there are many controversial areas of research – which are often the most interesting and challenging. This book, as well as giving basic facts and well accepted theories, gives the reader a taste of some of the exciting new discoveries that have been made, and a few glimpses of the new horizons that are beginning to appear.

Brain and Mind

The adult human brain is a walnut-shaped object roughly the size of a small cantaloupe. It weighs approximately three and a half pounds and has the consistency of thick porridge. The brain is probably the most complex object in the known universe. It is made up of about one hundred billion nerve cells, which are grouped into many distinct patterns. Nerve cells in some areas of the brain receive messages from the senses and from organs within the body. While receiving all this information, the brain is also sending out a constant stream of messages to all parts of the body, the skeleton, muscles, glands and other organs. It controls every action a person makes as well as the body's internal functions.

People often describe the mind as the sum of all conscious thoughts, perceptions and feelings. Most scientists who study the mind, and psychologists in particular, think that it is much more than that because it contains many processes of which people are not conscious. Take, for example, our store of memories. Although people can store memories in the mind for a long time, they are not conscious of a particular memory until they actually recall it. The mind also contains a great deal of knowledge that they can never consciously examine. Speech is a good example of this. No one can speak intelligibly or understand the speech of others without acquiring the rules of grammar. The infant is learning grammatical rules from the moment it tries to speak, but even adults are not normally aware of the grammatical rules they have unconsciously learned. People also have the ability to understand the behavior of others, yet they can seldom explain how they do it. Indeed, they often do not even know the real reason why they act in a particular way themselves.

Philosophers, psychologists and brain scientists have long puzzled over the relationship between mind and brain. The brain works in an orderly physical way, and the substances in the brain obey the laws of physics and chemistry. When different parts of the brain are injured, predictable changes in thinking or behavior occur. Drugs and electrical stimulation affect the brain and can cause changes in mood or alter people's ability to understand what is happening

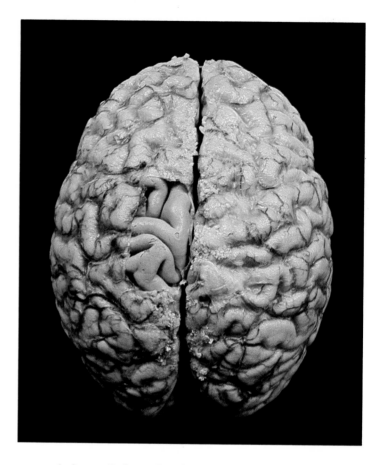

around them. It has also been discovered that some experiences – for instance, stress – can cause changes in the chemistry of the brain. These changes can, in turn, cause alterations of mood. Thus the brain both controls behavior and is itself affected by external events. When we think about this, we face the ancient and still baffling questions: what is consciousness and do people have, in any real sense, free will?

Although scientists have discovered many of the brain's activities underlying sensation, emotions and basic drives, they are still far from a full understanding of what consciousness really is or why it arose in the course of evolution. Being aware of the world around us makes it possible for us to consider different courses of action and choose between them. It may be that the nature of consciousness will be the last mystery to be solved by the human mind – if it ever is solved.

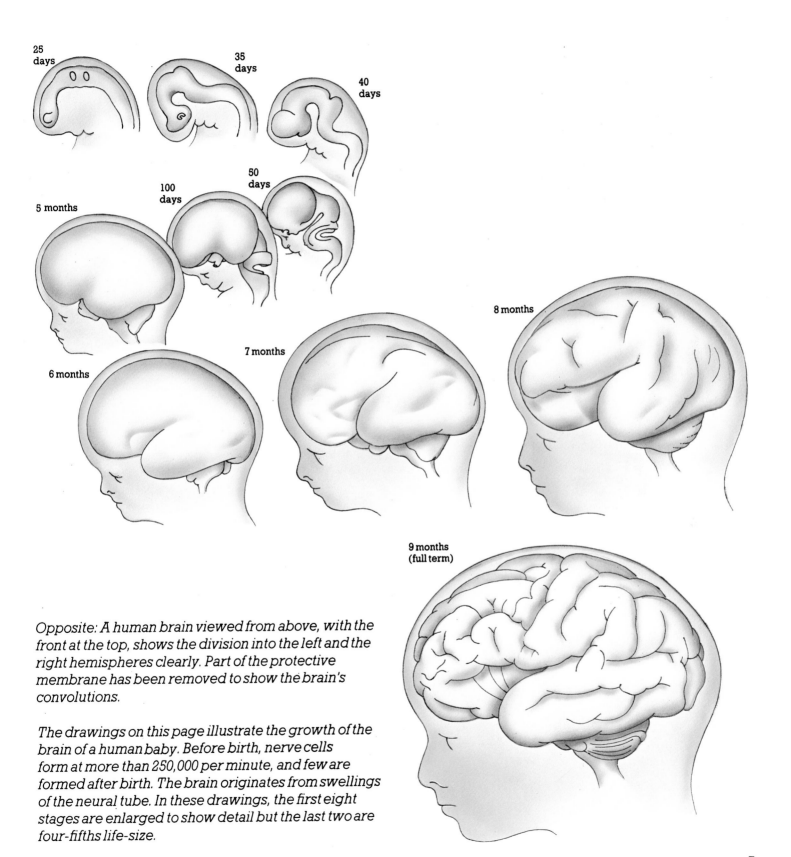

25 days

35 days

40 days

50 days

100 days

5 months

6 months

7 months

8 months

9 months (full term)

Opposite: A human brain viewed from above, with the front at the top, shows the division into the left and the right hemispheres clearly. Part of the protective membrane has been removed to show the brain's convolutions.

The drawings on this page illustrate the growth of the brain of a human baby. Before birth, nerve cells form at more than 250,000 per minute, and few are formed after birth. The brain originates from swellings of the neural tube. In these drawings, the first eight stages are enlarged to show detail but the last two are four-fifths life-size.

Psychology as a Science

Psychology is often defined as the study of behavior. Like other sciences, it has developed through research, that is by carefully planned investigations performed to achieve a precise understanding of events. Psychology is unlike other sciences because its subject matter is people and everyone feels that he has a personal knowledge of how his mind works. However, everyday descriptions of behavior lack the precision of scientific explanations. People use terms that they cannot define exactly, and they take a great deal for granted. Thus, the statement "She opened the kitchen door because she felt hungry" is a scientifically inadequate explanation of why the woman entered the kitchen. It leaves a lot of questions unanswered. How is the information about where food can be found stored in her mind? How is this information recalled when it is needed? How does the woman plan a series of actions that will enable her to find food? What mechanisms govern walking? How is a doorknob recognized and how does vision control the arm and hand that operates the knob? What are the internal and external events that control hunger?

By performing systematic experiments on behavior psychologists can discover a great deal about how memory and vision work, and about the factors governing hunger. In some cases psychologists may be able to put this information together with discoveries about the brain and thus identify the detailed brain processes underlying behavior. In other cases they may be able to work out the logical steps the brain must go through in order to control human actions, but be unable to discover the detailed physiological processes.

Reaching a decision – even a simple decision such as where to find food – always involves solving a problem. In solving a problem the brain makes a series of logical steps that are similar to the steps made in a computer program. For this reason, psychologists often write programs that are intended to model the steps taken by the brain in solving a particular problem. By running the program on a computer and discovering whether it really can solve the problem, a psychologist can discover whether his program really explains how people solve similar problems. Often the program does not run correctly the first time. The psychologist can learn from this failure and then rewrite his program.

To understand a program, the programmer needs to follow through the sequence of logical steps it carries out. But he does not need to know which part of the

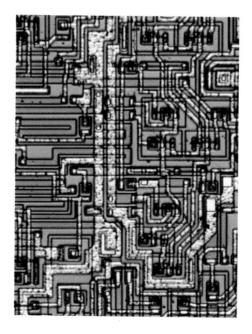 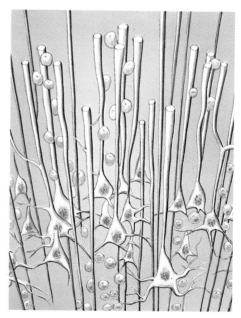

On the right is a microchip circuit often used in watches. Switches in it are turned on and off at five billionths of a second. On the far right is a group of nerve cells, the brain's own switches, which take about one thousandth of a second to operate. The microchip is faster but the brain's functions far surpass the performance of the microchip.

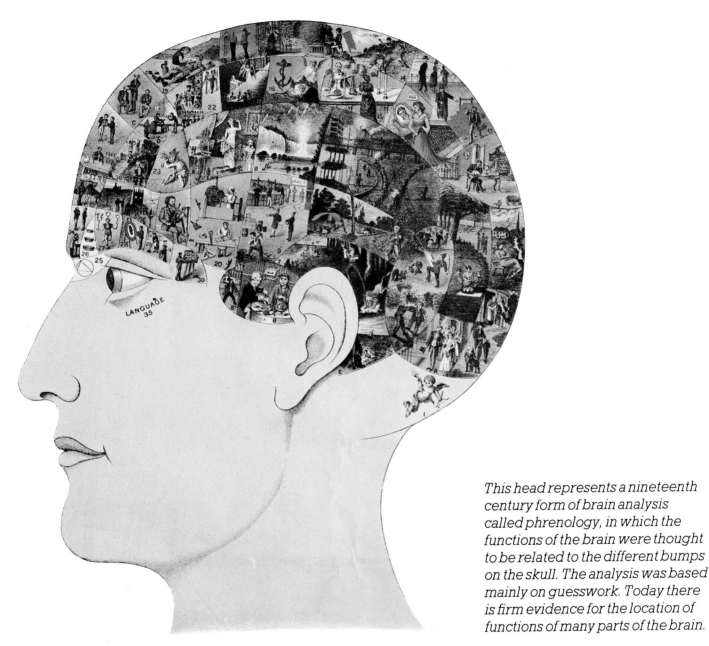

LANGUAGE
35

This head represents a nineteenth century form of brain analysis called phrenology, in which the functions of the brain were thought to be related to the different bumps on the skull. The analysis was based mainly on guesswork. Today there is firm evidence for the location of functions of many parts of the brain.

computer is responsible for carrying out each step. Similarly, an experimental psychologist can try to identify the programs that are run in the brain without knowing which nerve cells are carrying out each step. Although scientists would eventually like to know both the logical steps conducted by the mind and how the nervous system is wired up to carry them out, they realize that the wiring of the brain is so complicated that it may never be fully understood.

In addition to experimental psychologists, others work in different branches of psychology, applying scientific knowledge to real life. Many now work in industry. Occupational psychologists may investigate how physical and social environments cause stress in employees and managers, and discover aptitudes for different jobs. Clinical psychologists work closely with other health professionals. They see people of all ages, giving psychological treatment or administering tests to check brain functions and assess intelligence. Educational psychologists work in schools with children who have learning or behavior problems. They often give some psychological treatment and advise and counsel both parents and teachers. Social psychologists carry out research on the interaction between people. Some of them work with official bodies and help to make social policy.

What the Brain Does

By studying man's evolutionary history, scientists have increased our understanding of how man's brain works. As life on earth gradually became more complex, creatures needed to develop a sophisticated control center for all their bodily functions. Scientists can learn a great deal about these control systems, or brains, both by studying simple animals that exist today and also by looking at the bones and fossil records left in the earth by animals that existed in the past. It is known that the brain of man is the most well developed of all animal brains. According to the theory of the triune (three-in-one) brain, if evolutionary history is correctly understood people today appear to have a record of the brain's evolutionary development within their skulls. There appear to be not one but three control systems there.

The three brain areas – hindbrain, midbrain and forebrain – do not correspond exactly to past animal brains, but gives clues to early stages of evolution. The hindbrain is similar to the brain of reptiles, which dominated the earth millions of years before man appeared. The midbrain is similar to the brain of the lower animals that replaced reptiles, and the forebrain is like that of the most recently evolved mammals. In evolutionary terms, the hindbrain and midbrain have changed little with the passage of time, but the cortex of the forebrain of man is the result of spectacular development that was apparently accomplished by half a million years ago.

The hindbrain is the control center for basic involuntary reflexes, those actions, such as breathing, that people hardly ever think about, but that keep them alive. The midbrain regulates activities that must be done in sequence, such as avoiding danger or finding and consuming food. It also controls emotions and the drives necessary for reproduction. The forebrain, the most highly developed human brain structure, is literally our thinking cap. It is the seat of reason and overlays the more animal-like functions of the hind- and midbrain. The three sections must work together to achieve our needs, and they are anatomically interconnected along many nerve pathways, which in turn connect the brain with every other part of the body.

The brain does its work by receiving information from all the internal and external senses. This information is then converted into electrical impulses, which are passed from one nerve cell to the next. Some bodily systems communicate with the brain chemically. Chemicals called hormones pass to nerve cells in the brain through the bloodstream. Once there, they affect the number of electrical impulses produced by different nerve cells. These impulses may in turn initiate other chemical changes, or may activate different brain areas.

Scientists discover how the brain works by using three main techniques. The oldest, and still an essential

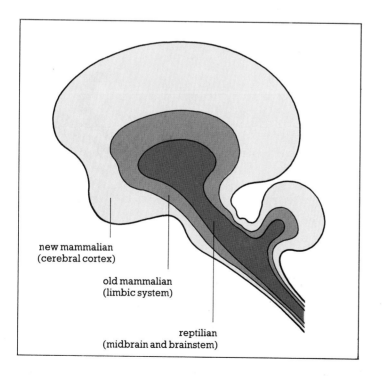

new mammalian
(cerebral cortex)

old mammalian
(limbic system)

reptilian
(midbrain and brainstem)

This diagram illustrates the triune brain theory developed by Paul MacLean of the National Institute of Mental Health in the United States. The brain developed layers in successive periods in the evolution of life on earth, as reptiles and warm-blooded animals appeared. These brain layers correspond roughly to human fore-, mid-, and hindbrain.

method, is to observe what happens to a person when the brain is injured. Another method is to make and study recordings of the electrical impulses that the brain produces. A third technique is to trace chemical substances as they pass from area to area within the brain as it works.

When scientists watch how the brain's capabilities develop in children and how it works in adults, they discover that the brain is designed to learn how to learn. Computer scientists often say that their machines carry out simple operations far more quickly than the brain. However, the brain – especially for activities such as thinking, vision and the use of language – has capabilities far beyond any present-day computer.

Guests at a banquet, like the one below held for Nobel Prize winners in Sweden, use various areas of the brain as they fulfill a basic need – eating – while engaging in complex social behavior.

Viktor Korchnoi, during a chess championship, is silent and motionless, but many areas of his brain are working to solve a problem and exclude unimportant aspects of his environment.

Nerve Cells

A cell is the smallest unit of the body that can function independently and that can be said to be alive. The nervous system, which includes the brain, the spinal cord and all the nerves in the body, is made up of nerve cells, called neurons. The vast majority of neurons in the nervous system are of a type called intermediary neruons, or interneurons. Like all cells, neurons are enclosed by a thin outer sheet of living matter, a membrane. This membrane preserves the cell's shape, regulates the entry of the chemicals that the cell needs to function, and regulates the elimination of the cell's waste products. A typical neuron has three parts: the cell body, the dendrites and axon. A dendrite is a tiny, twig-like structure branching out from the cell body. The cell body is roughly spherical and contains the cell's nucleus, which controls the chemical activity of the neuron. The axon is a long, thin tube that emerges from the cell body and divides at its far end into many different branches, whose terminals make

contact with the dendrites and cell bodies of other neurons. Some, but not all, axons have a special insulation called myelin. Most of the axons in the brain are microscopic, but others in the body can be more than a yard long.

The signal produced by most nerve cells is an electrical impulse, which begins in the cell body and is transmitted along the axon to its terminals. When this happens scientists say the cell is excited or firing. With two exceptions, a neuron fires when sufficient impulses from other cells reach its dendrites or cell body within a short time span. The excited cell will, in turn, influence the firing of many other cells, which are in contact with the terminals of its axon. Most cells transmit impulses in one direction only, and the size of the impulse is always the same for a given cell. The number of impulses transmitted in a second can vary. The more impulses the cell receives from other cells, the more frequently it fires. The electric impulse travels

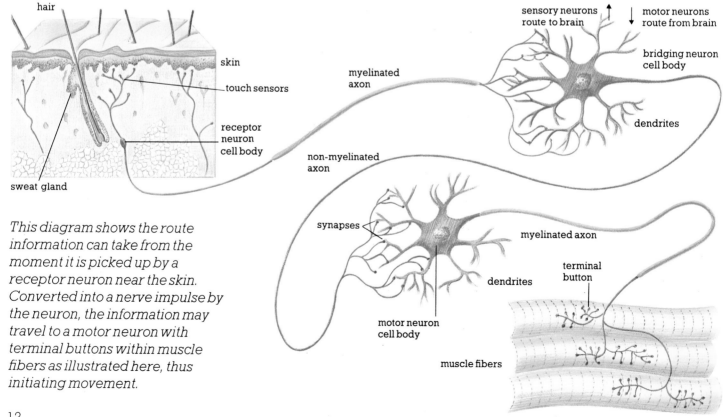

This diagram shows the route information can take from the moment it is picked up by a receptor neuron near the skin. Converted into a nerve impulse by the neuron, the information may travel to a motor neuron with terminal buttons within muscle fibers as illustrated here, thus initiating movement.

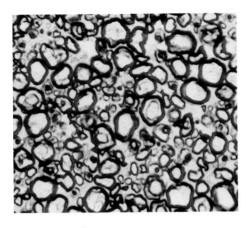

This electron micrograph shows a section cut through hundreds of nerve fiber axons.

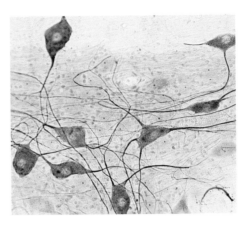

This electron micrograph reveals motor neuron cell bodies and their axons in the intestine.

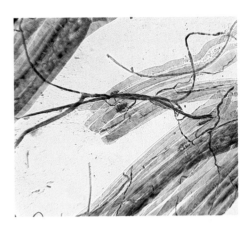

At high magnification we see thread-like neurons activating tubes of muscle fiber.

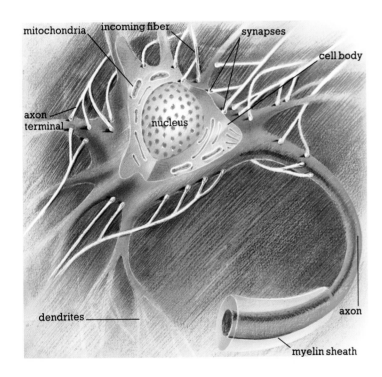

The nerve cell above is a typical basic unit of the nervous system. The cell body contains the nucleus, which controls the neuron's electrochemical activity. Mitochondria provide energy for the cell. Some axons, like the one shown, are protected by a myelin sheath, which insulates the axon from surrounding axons and speeds the passage of electrical impulses. Incoming fibers from other cells are shown in white.

along a given axon at a fixed speed. Because conducting impulses takes time, no one can react instantly to a signal from the outside world. It is for this reason that when a pedestrian suddenly walks into the street in front of a car it takes a driver at least a quarter of a second before he slams on the brakes.

In addition to the interneurons, which both fire other neurons and are fired by them, there are two specialized types of neurons, sensory cells and motor cells. Sensory cells are fired by changes in energy outside the nervous system. Certain cells in the eye, called receptors, for example, contain chemical substances that change the energy of light into electrical excitation. They trigger sensory cells that signal the presence of light to the brain. Other sensory cells are sensitive to sound, to pressure on the skin or to changes of temperature. Many sensory cells respond not to what is happening outside the body, but to events inside the body, such as changes in blood pressure and muscle tension.

Motor cells are fired by other neurons too, but their terminals end on a muscle or a gland instead of another neuron. When motor cells fire, they make the muscle contract or the gland secrete the substance it contains. Apart from the well-known glands, such as the sweat glands, the body contains many others that secrete chemicals known as hormones into the bloodstream. Hormones change the activity of organs and also influence the working of the brain itself.

Synapses and Neurotransmitters

The place where one neuron influences the firing of another is called a synapse. It acts like a switch that can route a signal through or stop it. The neuron ending at the synapse is called pre-synaptic, and the one to which it passes signals is called post-synaptic. The cell body and dendrites of most neurons have hundreds of synapses that influence their activities. Electrical impulses generated by nerve cells can be routed in many different ways, depending on how the switches, or the synapses, are connected.

A pre-synaptic neuron can increase or decrease the probability of the post-synaptic nerve cell firing. Such increases are called excitation and the decreases, inhibition. The delicate balance between the amounts of excitation and inhibition determines whether or not the post-synaptic neuron fires. Signals are transmitted along the axon electrically, but communication between different nerve cells is carried out by chemicals passing from one to another across the synapses. It is as though one neuron influences the next by spitting chemicals at it. This chemical bridge adds an extra dimension to the neuron's capabilities. At present, about forty of these message-carrying chemicals, known as neurotransmitters, have been identified, but there are probably more. There are often different transmitters at work in different systems of the brain, but some transmitters work in numerous systems. The transmitters in those parts of the brain controlling anxiety are different from those controlling hunger. In this way different systems are kept apart, even though two or more systems may overlap within the brain. In a further complication, a single neuron can use several transmitters. Although the brain as a whole is extremely complex, there is no confusion among its different systems.

Here is an outline of how a synapse works. The terminals of a pre-synaptic axon contain tiny sacks called vesicles, which store individual droplets of a single neurotransmitter. When an electrical impulse

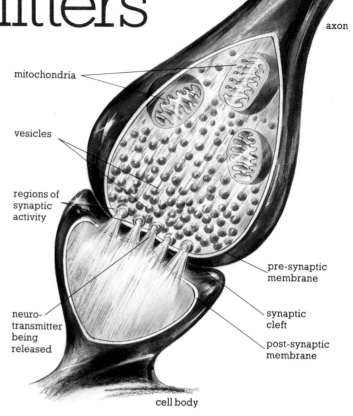

This diagram shows how chemicals called neurotransmitters cross the cleft at a synapse, the point of contact between an axon and a cell body. The chemicals are released into the cleft from special storage vesicles.

reaches the axon terminal of the pre-synaptic neuron, the vesicles fuse with the cell membrane and then open to release their contents into the gap between the two cells, called the synaptic cleft. On the surface of the membrane of the post-synaptic cell, facing the cleft, are special receptor sites. The molecules of the neurotransmitter slot into these sites like pieces of a biochemical jigsaw puzzle and bind onto the receptors. The presence of the neurotransmitter then either excites or inhibits the firing of the post-synaptic cell. After the neurotransmitter has done its work, it is removed by either being pumped back into the vesicles or

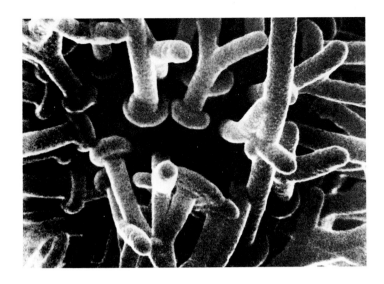

The photograph above shows the large number of axons making synaptic connections with just one nerve cell body.

destroyed while still in the cleft by other chemicals called enzymes. This clears the pathway for new messages to be transmitted.

Such a complicated system can go wrong in many ways. Neurotransmitters are manufactured within the pre-synaptic cell from substances the cell gathers in from the blood. Irregularities at this stage mean that too little or too much neurotransmitter may be produced. Sometimes there are too many or too few receptor sites on the post-synaptic cell itself. When this happens the cell will fire inappropriately, for example too often or too seldom. When neurotransmitters in the synaptic cleft are removed either too quickly or too slowly, this, too, causes messages to be distorted, and harmful consequences can occur. If the receptor sites in neurons that control someone's vital organs are blocked, the person will die. Curare, a well-known poison, imitates a neurotransmitter and jams the receptor sites of neurons controlling the muscles. They cannot receive their appropriate neurotransmitters, and therefore they cannot contract. The victim is paralyzed, and because the diaphragm cannot work, he stops breathing and dies.

Some of the best understood neurotransmitters are dopamine, enkephalins and endorphins, epinephrine, norepinephrine serotonin and acetylcholine. They are involved in different brain activities, such as the regulation of mood, the perception of pain and the control of muscular activity. Some illnesses, such as Parkinson's disease, are caused by faults in individual neurotransmitter systems. As scientists come to understand neurotransmitters better, they can develop better drugs to help treat illnesses of this kind.

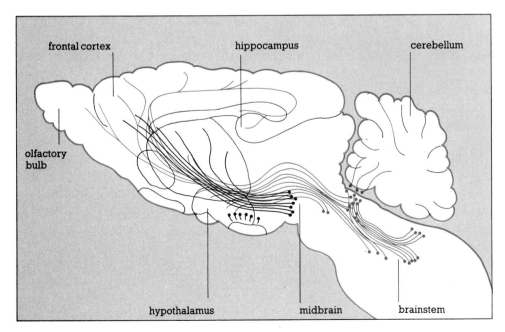

On the left, the pathways of the neurotransmitters dopamine (black) and norepinephrine (red) are mapped in the brain of a laboratory rat. The circuits shown here are involved in learning and reward, as well as motivation.

Parts of the Brain

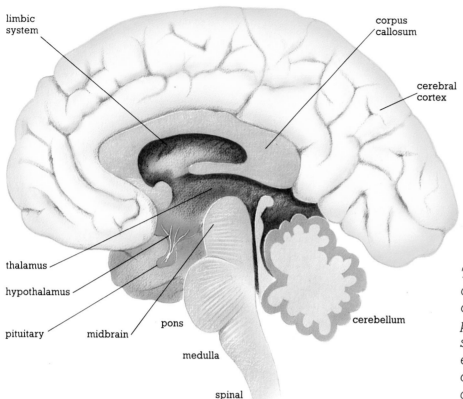

limbic system

corpus callosum

cerebral cortex

thalamus

hypothalamus

pituitary

midbrain

pons

cerebellum

medulla

spinal cord

This drawing of the right hemisphere of the brain shows the three main divisions of the brain and their relative positions: the brainstem, the limbic system and the cerebral cortex. Within each division there are several clearly defined structures. Others merge into one another and all interact.

Each division of the brain – hindbrain, midbrain and forebrain – contains many specialized areas and is connected by many different nervous pathways to the other divisions.

As the spinal cord enters the skull, it enlarges to form the medulla, an important part of the hindbrain. The connections from the spinal cord pass through the medulla to reach other parts of the brain. Immediately above the medulla is the pons, appropriately named because that is the Latin word for bridge. The medulla and the pons control the actions called involuntary reflexes, such as heart beat, blood pressure and breathing. Damage to these areas usually causes death. The vital nerve pathways ascending to higher brain centers pass through the pons. Near the medulla and pons is a dense collection of nerves called the reticular activating system (RAS). When excited, the RAS increases alertness. It also plays a role in directing

attention. Working to balance the RAS during deep sleep is the raphe system in the same region. The remaining part of the hindbrain is the cerebellum, which plays a role in coordinating body movements. If the cerebellum is damaged, the patient tends to make jerky, badly coordinated movements.

Above the hindbrain is the midbrain, which is a comparatively small structure. Connections from all parts of the hindbrain pass through the midbrain to reach the forebrain. The midbrain contains centers that receive information from the eyes and ears, and it plays a part in controlling eye movements.

The largest of the three primary divisions is the forebrain. At its base is the hypothalamus. Although the hypothalamus is only about the size of a pea, it is vital for life. It regulates hunger and thirst, temperature control and sex. It also affects how anxious or aggressive people feel. Damage to one part of it causes

The hippocampus and the amygdala are two of the many parts of the limbic system; the former plays an important role in memory and the latter plays a similarly important role in aggression.

Close to the limbic system is the thalamus. This is the brain's great relay center and works together with many other areas of the brain. The thalamus is involved in almost all aspects of behavior. Parts of it are connected with the limbic system and hence are involved in emotion. The thalamus also receives messages from the eyes, ears and other senses, and routes them to the appropriate part of the cerebral cortex, the brain's outer layer. The descending pathways from the cerebral cortex to the muscles also pass through the thalamus. The cortex therefore plays a part in controlling movement and has connections to the cerebellum. The cortex covers the cerebrum, which is divided into two cerebral hemispheres and is the most prominent part of the human brain.

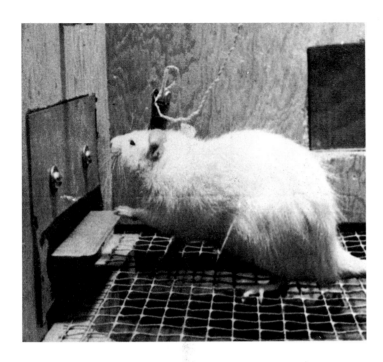

Above is a laboratory rat with an electrode surgically implanted deep in the center of the brain in one area of its hypothalamus. Electrical stimulation here and in other "reward centers" produces feelings of intense pleasure. This reward is so great that the rat quickly learns to press a lever to obtain it and will ignore food or opportunities for sex to continue enjoying this stimulation.

weight gain; damage to another causes weight loss. A tumor pressing on another part may cause extreme irritability. The hypothalamus also controls the pituitary gland, which lies below the base of the brain. This gland secretes many different hormones, some of which control other glands within the body. Much recent research into how the pituitary gland works suggests that it may play an important role in the way people react to fear or stress.

The hypothalamus is closely connected with the limbic system, which helps to control the emotions. Damage to the limbic system may cause depression, apathy and irritability. It contains centers that, when stimulated by small electric shocks, cause feelings of extreme pleasure or anxiety and panic. Stimulating these pleasure or reward centers in controlled laboratory experiments with animals has given scientists important clues as to how learning takes place.

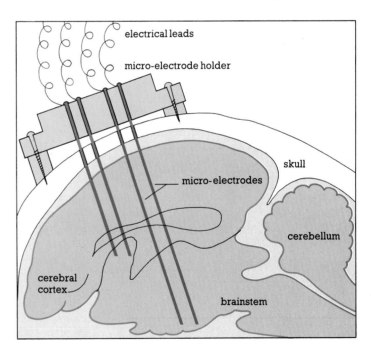

The diagram above shows how microelectrodes are implanted in the brains of laboratory animals for experiments involving electrical stimulation of the brain. A mild electrical current passes through the microelectrode directly into the area in the brain being studied. The animal's reactions to the electrical stimulation give scientists information about the role the stimulated area plays in the brain.

The Cerebral Cortex

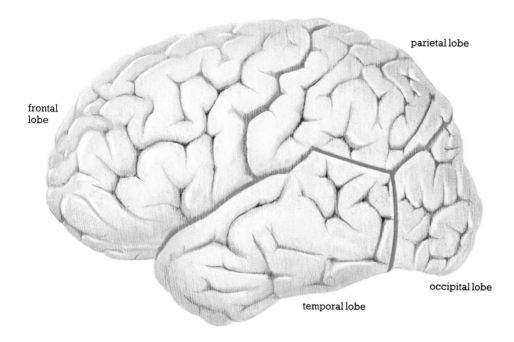

parietal lobe

frontal lobe

occipital lobe

temporal lobe

This side view of the brain shows the four lobes of the left half of the cerebral cortex. The lobes were named after the occipital, parietal, temporal and frontal bones of the skull, which they lie under. The right half of the cortex is divided into the same four lobes.

The cerebral cortex, a sheet of cells about a quarter of an inch thick, covers the top and sides of each half of the brain and folds down between them. It is deeply wrinkled and these wrinkles give the surface of the brain its characteristic crumpled appearance. Laid out flat, the cerebral cortex could cover more than two square feet. Its wrinkles enable this large area to be packed inside the skull. All complex mental activity appears to depend on the cerebral cortex. This is the part of the brain we often call our gray matter. No animal has a cortex as well developed as man's. By observing patients who have suffered injury or strokes damaging the cortex, and by experiments on animals, scientists have discovered a great deal about how it works. Some regions control movement, others receive messages from the senses, and much of it is devoted to language and thought. Those areas not concerned with the five senses, the body or movement, are called association cortex.

The cerebral cortex is split from front to back into two equal halves or hemispheres, which are linked in many ways but chiefly through a mass of nerves called the corpus callosum. Each hemisphere has four sec-

tions or lobes: occipital, parietal, temporal and frontal. Each lobe has two symmetrical halves, one in each hemisphere. The right side of the body is controlled by the left hemisphere and the left side by the right hemisphere. The occipital lobes receive messages from the eyes. A wound through a particular part of the occipital cortex causes blindness in the part of the eye to which it is connected.

At the side of each occipital lobe are the temporal lobes. The top sections receive messages from the ears. In most people the upper rear part of the left temporal lobe controls the comprehension of language. Speech production is largely controlled by the lower rear area of the left frontal lobe. The lower parts of the temporal lobes are essential for memory and for the visual recognition of objects.

The parietal lobes are also important in recognition, particularly of faces. People with damage to them have difficulty finding their way around or understanding and using maps. At the front of the parietal lobes is a vertical strip, the somatosensory cortex, which receives sense messages from the skin and muscles. Information is received here about heat, cold, touch

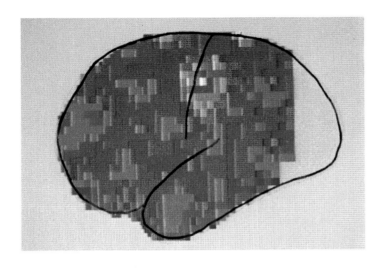

This blood flow picture of the right hemisphere, made while the subject was moving his left hand rhythmically, shows – red and yellow – the somatosensory strip to be the most active area.

and pain. Here also the sensations of our bodily movements are monitored.

At the rear of the frontal lobes is another strip, the motor cortex, which is parallel with the somatosensory cortex. It triggers voluntary movements. A large part of both these strips is devoted to the face, which is understandable when we think about the number of tiny muscle movements made by the face. Most of the frontal lobes are association cortex. They play an important role in organized thinking. Damage to the front part of the frontal lobes can make people incapable of forming and carrying out plans. Through their connections with the limbic system these lobes are also involved in emotion.

Despite the importance of the cerebral cortex, it does nothing on its own. It works in collaboration with all other brain areas, and there is a constant scurrying of nerve impulses between the cerebral cortex and other brain centers.

Homunculus ("little man") drawings show where parts of the body are governed in the somatosensory and motor strips of the cortex.

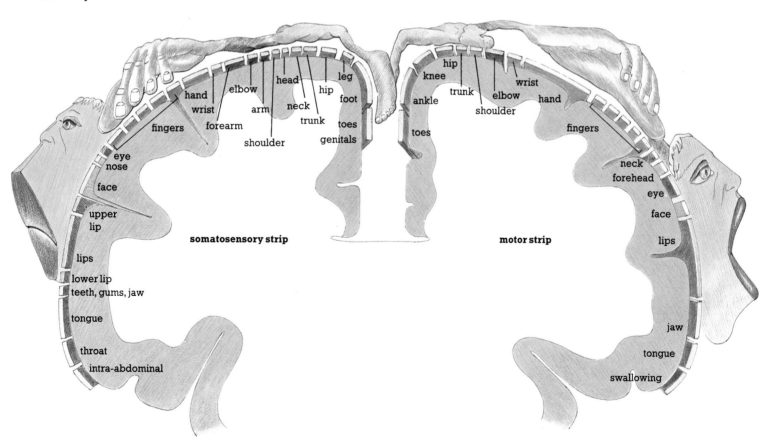

Left Brain, Right Brain

As early as the 1860s doctors began to suspect that the two cerebral hemispheres, especially the left and right cerebral cortex, might have different functions. They observed that right-handed patients who had suffered damage to the left half of the brain by a stroke or head injury tended to have problems in the use and understanding of language. Later it was discovered that in left-handed people the language centers are usually either in the right half of the cortex or are located on both sides. Most adults whose language centers are damaged never recover the full use of language. However, a child who receives severe damage to the left hemisphere before the age of four or five often develops normal speech and understanding. The right hemisphere appears to take over the language function of the left.

Some other abilities are also unevenly distributed between the hemispheres. In particular, the right hemisphere tends to be better than the left at recognizing complex objects such as faces, and is more important for musical ability. Patients with damage to their left hemisphere may be unable to speak, but they can still sing and dance. Some psychologists believe that the left hemisphere contains rational and logical abilities, while the right governs the more intuitive and emotional side of life. Although both sides of the brain are involved in emotions, emotions are more readily displayed on the left side of the face, controlled by the right hemisphere.

Roger Sperry, an American psychologist, won a Nobel prize in 1981 for his pioneering work on the role of the two hemispheres. He observed patients who, because of severe epilepsy, had brain operations in which the massive nerve bundle connecting the hemispheres, the corpus callosum, was cut. This "split-brain" operation was carried out to prevent epileptic seizures spreading from one hemisphere to the other. The operations usually reduced epileptic attacks and had few long term side effects. Immediately after the operations, however, the two hemispheres sometimes seemed to work completely independently. The patient might try to undress himself with his left hand, while trying to dress himself with his right. Such effects

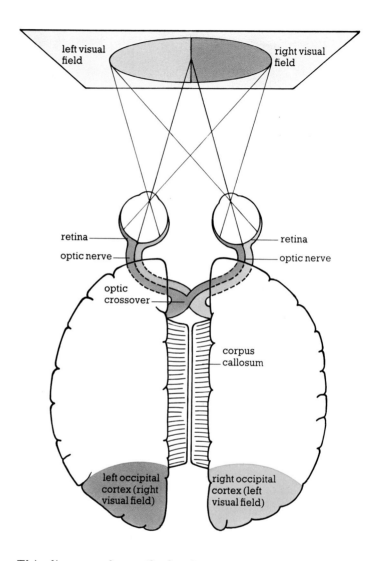

This diagram shows the basic sensory connections between the eyes and the areas at the rear of each half of the cerebral cortex that receives and interprets the information they send. Within each eye, the lens transposes the image, so that the right field of vision is registered on the left part of the retina and the left field of vision is registered on the right part of the retina. This transposition is continued in part by the major crossover of nerves just in front of the corpus callosum. That is, the right half of the left retina and the left half of the right retina send their information to the opposite sides of the brain.

LEFT HEMISPHERE	RIGHT HEMISPHERE
language and memory	
control of spontaneous speech	swearing
writing	drawing of geometric shapes
determines reply to verbal commands	responds to simple commands
word recognition	face recognition
memory for words and numbers	memory for shapes and music
	repetition of simple words
perception and thought	
control of sequential movements	dressing correctly
	contributes to map reading skills
	control of rotating mental images
sensation and movement	
sensory input mostly from right side of environment	sensory input mostly from left side of environment
control of fine movements of right hand	control of the fine movements of left hand
control of playacting movements	
control of complex movements	
ability to name fingers	

The chart above lists differences in specialized function between the two hemispheres of the human cerebral cortex. Most of this information has been obtained by studying the problems that people have with speech, memory and movement after receiving injuries to one or other hemisphere. Some skills do not affect the quality of life, but others, such as understanding speech, are vital.

soon disappeared, but more subtle results could still be detected. Split-brain patients whose language centers were in the left hemisphere were asked to identify a pen and other small objects by feeling them. When the pen was presented to the right hand, the patients were able to say "That's a pen" because nerve fibers from the right hand run to the left (language) hemisphere. When the pen was presented to the left hand (right brain), the patients could not say what it was, but they could still recognize it. They would make writing movements with their left hand (controlled by the right hemisphere), and could even draw the pen correctly with that hand. The right hemisphere was able to identify the pen, but was not able to describe it in words.

This type of experiment raises the question whether a split-brain patient's hemispheres are independently conscious. Since it does not control speech, the right side cannot tell us it is conscious. It seems possible that in such patients some independent consciousness is located in each hemisphere. For example, one patient had some language ability in both hemispheres. Although his right hemisphere could not control speech, it could spell out words with alphabet tiles. His hemispheres seemed to have different opinions. When asked what job he would most like to do, he replied, using the left hemisphere, "A draftsman," but using his right hemisphere, he spelled out "automobile race" with the alphabet tiles.

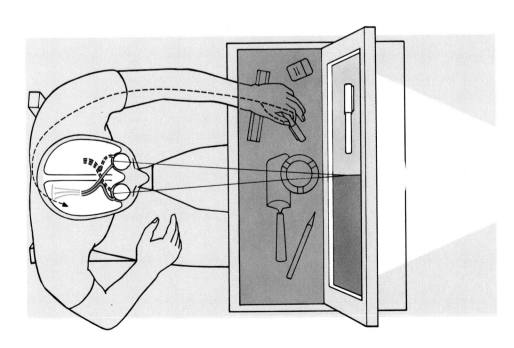

In the drawing at the left, a split-brain patient carries out a matching task to test his right hemisphere, the less verbal half of the brain. Staring straight ahead, he sees an image briefly flashed on the left screen. Unable to say its name, he can still try to match it with one of the objects hidden in the shelf below by using his left hand. To check his left brain, he can be asked to name the objects he sees or feels with his right hand.

Vision

The eyes are the receiving stations of the mind's most sophisticated information gathering system. They are the first link in a chain that collects and analyzes information from light waves. The information passes to the visual cortex, where many of the processes underlying visual perception occur.

Light is admitted to the eye through a small flexible opening at the front of the eye, the pupil. The pupil contracts in bright light to prevent the eye from being dazzled and enlarges in dim light so that enough light is admitted for us to see. Light is brought into sharp focus on the back of the eye by the cornea and the eye's lens. The lens changes its curvature depending on the distance of the object being look at, in order to produce a sharp image. The light is focused on the retina, a layer of nerve cells at the back of the eye. Each retina has more than one hundred million receptor neurons. These receptors contain photopigments, chemical substances that absorb the energy of light. Further chemical changes convert the light energy into electrical acitivity in the receptors, which fire other neurons that convey signals to the brain.

The receptors are of two kinds, called rods and cones. The rods form the outer part of each retina. They are sensitive in dim light, but since they have only one photopigment, they cannot detect color. This is why

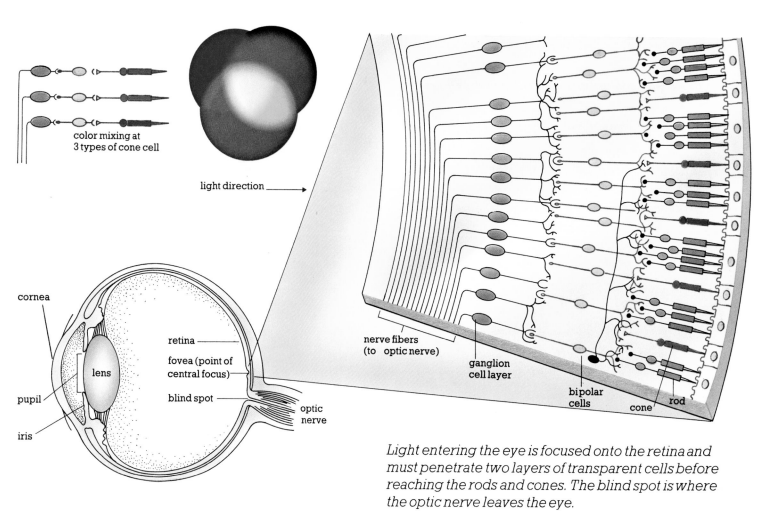

color mixing at
3 types of cone cell

light direction

cornea

lens

pupil

iris

retina

fovea (point of central focus)

blind spot

optic nerve

nerve fibers (to optic nerve)

ganglion cell layer

bipolar cells

cone

rod

Light entering the eye is focused onto the retina and must penetrate two layers of transparent cells before reaching the rods and cones. The blind spot is where the optic nerve leaves the eye.

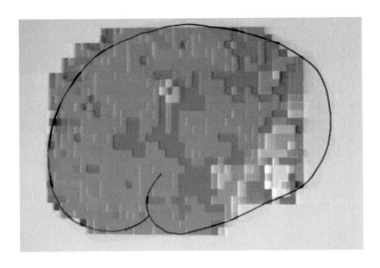

Blood flow in the occipital cortex, shown in red, is greatly increased when light is perceived. There is slight increased activity in the frontal eye field next to the motor strip of the frontal lobe.

you cannot see color in twilight when only the rods are working. The cones are concentrated in the center of the retina. There are three different kinds, each containing a different photopigment responding most strongly to a particular part of the spectrum – red, green or blue. Which color people see depends on the relative amount of stimulation each of the three kinds of cone receives. When each kind is stimulated equally, we perceive white.

Cones not only enable people to see color but, unlike rods, they are sensitive to fine detail. Because there is a decrease in the number of cones from the center of the retina outwards, we can see fine detail only in the center of our field of vision. If you fix your gaze on a single word on this page, you can make out only one or two words on either side of it. Our eyes swivel in the head so that by making eye movements we can bring different parts of the scene in succession onto the center of the retina in order to pick up the detail in each

Some examples of the variety of individual visual fields, near right, show how each causes different cells to fire. This depends on their shape, angle, and pattern of light and dark areas. Later in the process, far right, single cortical cells fire only to complete bars of light at particular angles. The cell illustrated fires most to a bar at the angle in C.

part. As you read this page, you are making between three and five eye movements a second.

It is very important to detect the changes in brightness that produce lines and edges since these mark the boundaries of objects and provide information about shape. David Hubel and Torsten Wiesel, working at Harvard University, won a Nobel prize in 1981 for their discovery of how the cells in the occipital cortex detect the presence of lines and edges. These cells have sometimes been called line and edge detectors and each is connected to a particular part of the retina. Different cells are fired by horizontal and vertical lines, and by lines in intermediate positions. Other cells respond to edges running across the visual field in certain directions. Some of these fire only if an image of a line or edge is moving across a specific part of the retina in a particular direction. Thus, lines and edges in different orientations and movement in different directions are processed at an early stage of the visual system. The pattern of lines and edges is then used to provide information about depth and to enable the observer to recognize objects.

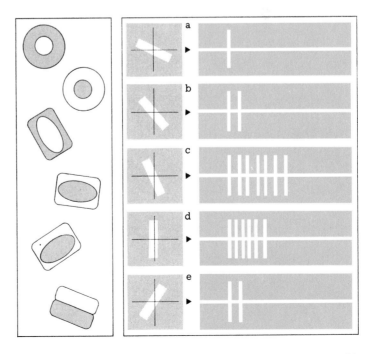

Visual Perception

Visual perception is the ability to judge distance and depth, to see motion, to recognize objects when seeing them at different distances or from different points of view, and to construct a model in our heads of the world around us. It would be impossible to walk around a room or pick up a pencil, let alone drive a car, without being able to judge distance. As in its performance of so many other tasks, the human brain uses several methods to judge distance, two of which depend on having two eyes. If you watch the eyes of a person shifting his gaze from a near to a far object, you will notice that the eyes move slightly apart. They move back towards one another as his gaze returns to a nearby object. These movements are needed to bring the object onto the exact center of each eye. The

farther apart the pupils are, the farther away the brain knows the object to be. But these movements of the eyes can tell the observer only his distance away from the object he is looking at. They must be used in conjunction with a second aspect of visual perception, called stereopsis, to obtain information about the relative distances away of various objects in the field of vision.

To understand stereopsis, hold your left index finger about a foot in front of your left eye. Keep both eyes on the finger, then open and close each in turn. The finger appears to move right when the left eye is opened and left when the right eye opens. Each eye has a different view of the world and the brain calculates the difference between these two views and uses it to perceive

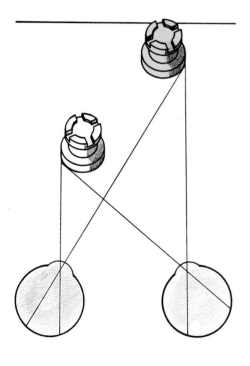

In stereoscopic vision, left, objects at different distances from the eyes stimulate unequal areas of the retinas. The brain averages the difference to judge the objects' distances and spatial relationship.

The principles of perspective were understood 2000 years ago, as a wall painting, above, from the Roman city of Pompeii, proves.

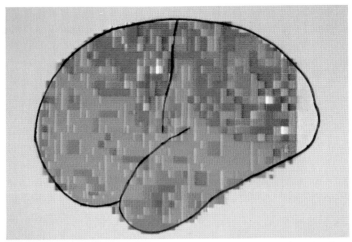

The red areas show that blood flow is increasing in the occipital cortex because the eyes are watching a moving object. Since many small complex movements of the head and eyes keep the image focused, the area close to the motor cortex is also very active.

The use of illusion to trick the eye is a popular theme for artists. In the 1915 cartoon the artist asks the reader to find the characters in his work entitled "My wife and my mother-in-law."

relative distance.

People with only one eye are still able to perceive depth, and everyone can see depth in a photograph or painting. One of the ways the brain does this is to use what it has learned about perspective as a clue to depth. Railway lines receding from the viewer gradually draw together on the eye and the brain interprets this to mean that they are going away. Again, if one object cuts off the view of another, the brain decides that the first object is in front of the second. Even the shape and position of shadows provide the brain with information about the three-dimensional nature of objects.

One of the most remarkable facts about vision is the ability to see things in their correct size, regardless of how far away they are from the observer. A person twenty feet away produces an image on the retina only one-fifth the size of the image of a person at four feet. Even young children show good size constancy. It is not known whether this skill is learned or inborn. To achieve size constancy the brain makes allowance for the distance at which the object is seen. Making use of the size of the object in the image, the brain then calculates its true size. In the same way colors are seen as constant in spite of different lighting conditions.

Another form of constancy concerns shape. For example, if you look at a saucer from above, the retinal image is round. From the side, it is oval. You would not say, as you moved to the side, that the saucer changed its shape. Shape constancy makes it possible to know the actual shape of an object regardless of the observer's point of view. When we move our eyes the image of the world sweeps across the retina, but we do not see the world move. The brain reads off the signal sent to move the eyes and cancels out the resulting motion on the retina.

From the information received as two-dimensional images on the retina, the brain constructs an accurate three-dimensional model of the scene and proceeds to recognize the objects within it.

Hearing and Attention

Hearing is one of the brain's most sophisticated abilities. People can understand speech only because they can accurately perceive pitch and loudness, which correspond to the frequency and intensity of the sound wave. In fact, through evolution man has acquired special mechanisms for perceiving speech, which are inborn. These mechanisms enable people to detect the subtle differences between different speech sounds.

The frequencies people can hear range from about thirty cycles a second up to about twenty thousand. High frequency sounds cannot be heard by older people and hearing generally is most acute at about one thousand cycles per second. Man also has the ability to concentrate selectively on a particular range of frequencies. If a person listens to two melodies played simultaneously, one in a high key, the other in a low, he can hear one or the other clearly, but cannot follow both at once. He can also focus his hearing on a single sound source, such as a friend's voice in a noisy crowd. This is called selective attention and is par-

ticularly important in a noisy environment. But even when people are concentrating on something, there are some special sounds that they find almost impossible to ignore. Think of your own reaction whenever you hear someone calling your name.

Sound is produced by rapid changes of air pressure, to which the structures of the ear are sensitive. Like a funnel, the outer ear – that is the visible part – channels the vibrations in the air towards the eardrum. The eardrum, a tight sheet of membrane, vibrates in step with changes in outside air pressure. Beyond it is the middle ear, which contains three tiny bones that amplify the vibrations and transmit them to the main hearing organ, a spiral tube called the cochlea. Down its center runs the basilar membrane, which is bathed in fluid.

When vibrations reach the basilar membrane, it goes into a wave-like motion, with high-pitched sounds affecting one end most and low sounds the other. These motions are detected by hair cells distributed along the membrane. The hair cells are the receptors for hearing. Through a series of intermediary neurons,

The diagrammatic cross section right through the human hearing apparatus shows how air is funneled into the eardrum by the visible part of the ear. Sound waves make the drum vibrate, and the vibrations are transmitted through the inner ear by three small bones. The vibrations move the stirrup bone against the oval window and this makes waves in the fluid that fills the cochlea canal. The round window allows the pressure wave to leave the cochlea once it has done its job.

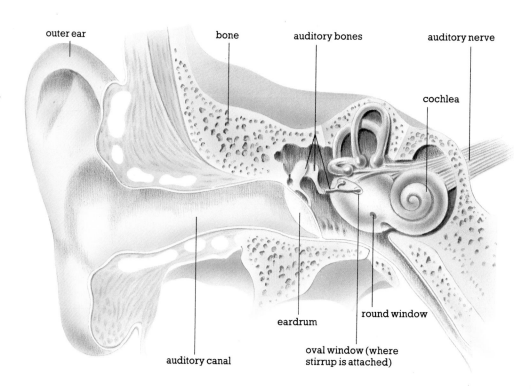

outer ear

bone

auditory bones

auditory nerve

cochlea

eardrum

round window

auditory canal

oval window (where stirrup is attached)

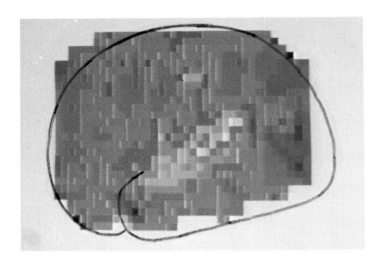

The blood flow picture left shows the excitation of the left temporal cortex in response to listening to music. The part known as Wernicke's area is most active but so too is the frontal eye field, which is possibly involved in locating sound in space.

they pass information to the medulla and to the temporal lobes. Little is known about how the temporal lobes process sound, but they probably deal mainly with its more complex aspects. The brain can analyze the different frequencies present in a sound wave and thus detect pitch. Injuries to the left temporal lobe usually cause severe problems in the perception and comprehension of speech.

It is important to be able to group together sounds that come from the same place. Clearly, early man living in the wild had to be able to concentrate on a single sound source to decide whether it was the call of an animal, a breaking twig or the approach of an enemy. If the brain dealt with all noises coming from all directions at once, people could not distinguish one sound from another and would hear only a confused and meaningless pattern.

The hearing system can lock onto a sound that comes from a particular direction and analyze it in detail while selectively disregarding sounds coming from other directions. The brain locates direction by two simple methods. If a sound comes from the left, it reaches the left ear a fraction of a second before it reaches the right one. The brain can measure this small difference in arrival time and thus estimate the sound's direction. The brain can also measure a gap of just over ten millionths of a second. It can also detect a minute difference in intensity and use that as a guide. A sound will be slightly weaker in the ear farther from the source because of the greater distance traveled. Localization of sound is thought to occur chiefly in the medulla.

The two children on the right are able to carry on a conversation in the deafening noise of a school dining room because of the brain's remarkable ability to pick out sounds selectively from a broad range of aural stimuli.

Smell, Taste, and Touch

Although people rely mainly on their eyes for finding out about the world around them and on their ears for obtaining information from other people, the remaining external senses – smell, taste and touch – also report significant events to the brain.

Our smell receptors, called osmoreceptors, lie high up in the nose. They detect the presence of airborne molecules and carry messages to the olfactory bulb, a small structure in the forebrain. From there, the signals pass to the cortex. Osmoreceptors have been identified and examined under a microscope, and scientists know that different osmoreceptors are triggered by the airborne molecules of different substances, but they do not know how many kinds of receptors there are or which molecules activate which osmoreceptors.

One substance to which these receptors are very sensitive is musk, which is secreted by many animals. The human nose can detect as little as one thousand billionth of an ounce in a pint of air. The concentration of wintergreen, another fragrant substance, must be ten million times as great before a person can smell it. The sensitivity to musk may have some evolutionary significance because it is possible that man's ancestors had to sense animals by smell, as well as by sight and hearing, in order to hunt them. In dogs, which are hunters, one-third of the cerebral cortex is devoted to

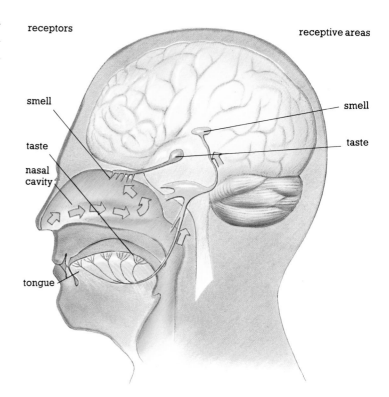

The osmoreceptors – receptors that detect airborne molecules – are estimated to be one thousand times more sensitive than receptors for taste. They are open to the air in the nasal cavity. In practice smell and taste work together, especially in our enjoyment of flavor.

The drawing on the right shows the distribution of the specialized taste buds on the tongue for bitter, sour, sweet and salty flavors. The microphotograph on the far right shows how each taste bud is set in a saliva-filled pit.

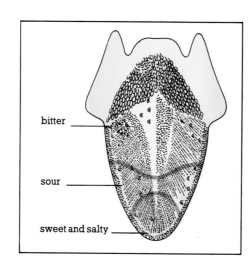

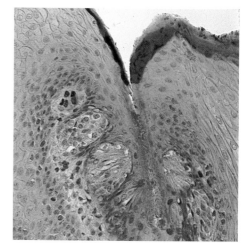

28

smell. Only one-twentieth of man's cortex is primarily concerned with smell.

Scientists know more about how taste works. There are about ten thousand taste buds in the mouth, most of which are scattered in four specialized areas on the tongue. Each taste bud has about fifteen or twenty receptor cells arranged like the segments of an orange around its tip. Individual buds have varing degrees of sensitivity to the four primary tastes: salty, sweet, sour and bitter. Taste is also affected by the temperature and the texture of food and by the way it stimulates the smell receptors. If you try, for example, to eat while pinching your nose, you will not be able to tell the difference between an apple and an onion, or between many other foods that you assume have very distinctive tastes. Scientists do not know how information from the taste buds is processed by the cortex.

The skin contains many receptors that are sensitive to external events, such as gentle touch, pressure, warmth and cold. The sensitivity of these senses varies considerably from one part of the body to another. Psychologists know little about the way people distinguish sensations. There are several different kinds of skin receptors, but often more than one kind is involved in detecting a given sensation. Scientists have learned, for example, that light pressure is picked up by receptors at the base of the tiny hairs in the skin, yet the lips are also sensitive to light pressure, and they are completely hairless. How a person detects heat is also mysterious. Using a tiny probe that is kept either hot or cold, scientists have found that there are separate receptors sensitive to heat and cold. These receptors are scattered at random over the surface of the skin, though there are more in the sensitive areas, such as the lips, than there are in the less sensitive regions, such as the back. Signals from the skin receptors are sent to the somatosensory cortex, that narrow band of cells at the front of the brain's parietal lobes. Scientists still have to discover exactly how this strip of cortex analyzes the signals it receives to enable people to perceive all the various skin sensations.

The reflex mechanism shown below diagrammatically, is just one example of a special link of sensory and motor neurons. If a toe is stubbed, sensory cells pass the message through another neuron to the motor cell that causes the leg muscles to contract. The foot can spring away quickly because the impulses governing such rapid movement do not need to travel to the brain and back, although the impulses are transmitted to the brain. Rapid reaction prevents further injury.

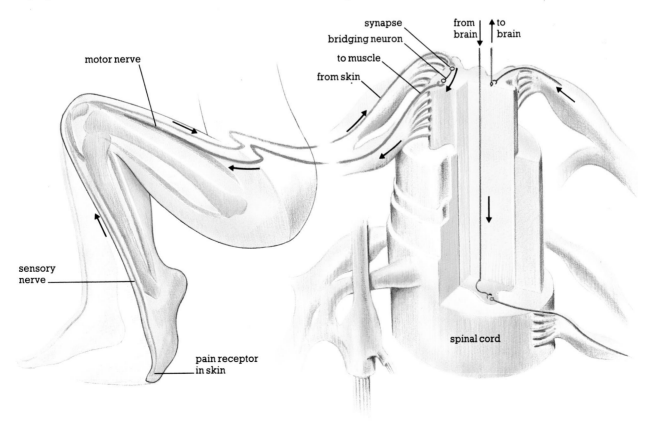

motor nerve

synapse
bridging neuron
to muscle
from skin
from brain
to brain

sensory nerve

pain receptor in skin

spinal cord

Speaking and Understanding

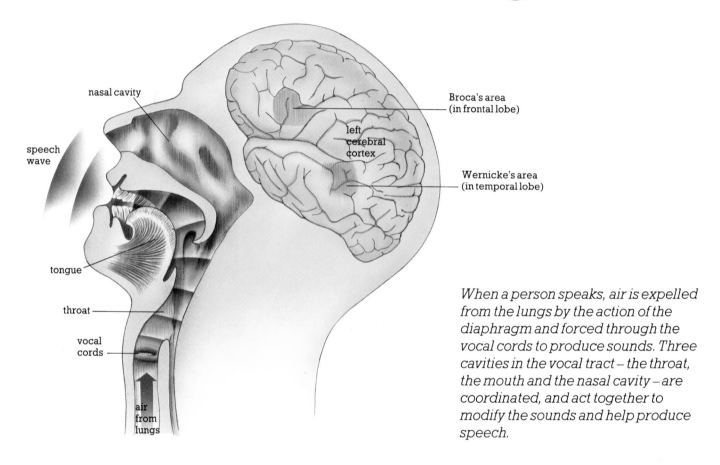

nasal cavity

speech wave

tongue

throat

vocal cords

air from lungs

Broca's area (in frontal lobe)

left cerebral cortex

Wernicke's area (in temporal lobe)

When a person speaks, air is expelled from the lungs by the action of the diaphragm and forced through the vocal cords to produce sounds. Three cavities in the vocal tract – the throat, the mouth and the nasal cavity – are coordinated, and act together to modify the sounds and help produce speech.

Man's capacity to speak depends on special evolutionary changes in the mouth and throat, and is associated with changes in the parts of the brain controlling speech and hearing. A cavity in the throat called the larynx contains the vocal cords. This pair of elastic membranes can be stretched taut by the muscles to which they are attached. When air is expelled from the lungs, it passes through the vocal cords, causing them to vibrate up and down rapidly. The vibration of the vocal cords produces sound. The rate at which the cords vibrate is the basic frequency of the voice, which in men is usually about one hundred pulses of air a second and in women, one hundred and sixty. The more tightly stretched the vocal cords, the higher the voice. In whispering, air is expelled through the throat and mouth, but because the cords are slack they do not vibrate.

Different syllables are produced by the changes made in the position of the tongue and the shape of the throat, nasal cavity and mouth, which are known collectively as the vocal tract. Air from the lungs makes various parts of the vocal tract vibrate. Depending on where the tongue is in the mouth and how the lips are formed, the vibrations have different frequencies. As the vibrations change, the sound produced changes. Each syllable of a word contains sounds of many

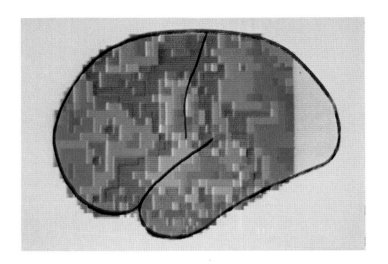

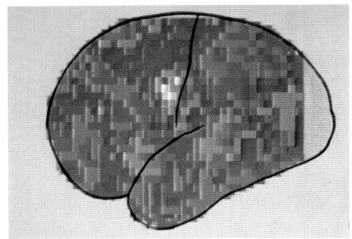

This picture of blood flow in the brain as someone counts shows that the pre-frontal cortex and the somatosensory and motor strips concerned with the mouth and vocal tract are active. Red in the temporal lobe is due to high flow because the person in this experiment is listening to his own voice. Broca's area does not require high flow because new speech patterns are not required.

The blood flow increases in the picture above take place in the lower temporal lobe, where hearing occurs, and are indicated in red. The subject in this experiment was reading aloud. Both Wernicke's and Broca's areas at the top of the temporal lobe and the bottom of the frontal lobe respectively, are clearly defined because both must act together to carry out this task successfully.

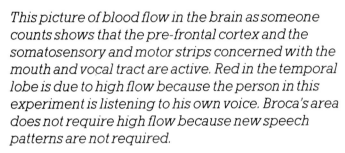

different frequencies.

When a vowel is spoken, the vocal cords vibrate. Consonants are produced in a different way, usually by interrupting the flow of air in some way. Bringing the lips together to produce "b" or "p" or putting the tongue behind the teeth to produce "t" or "d" are good examples. Some languages, in addition to vowels and consonants, have clicks – sounds made by drawing air into the mouth, pressing the tongue against the teeth or roof of the mouth, and then removing it suddenly.

Speech perception is very complex. When people talk, the speech wave travels through the air to the listener. The continuous stream of sound must be analyzed by the brain to recover the individual units that make up language. Although the listener hears gaps between words, no such pauses are present in the speech wave. Indeed, there are often longer periods of silence within a word than between words. Context helps the brain identify particular syllables or words. In an interesting experiment, speech was recorded and a complete syllable was removed from a sentence and replaced by a mechanical click. Listeners claimed to hear the missing syllable as if it were really there. They also heard the click, although they were not sure

at exactly which point it came. They could place it only to within four or five syllables of its correct position.

Different but connected parts of the brain, known as Broca's area and Wernicke's area after the nineteenth-century neurologists who discovered them, control and perceive speech. Broca's area governs the ability to produce intelligible speech and lies just in front of the place in the motor cortex where the muscles of the mouth and throat are controlled. If Broca's area is damaged, either by a stroke or injury, speech may become slow and poorly articulated. Many words are omitted, particularly pronouns and conjunctions, a condition called expressive aphasia.

Injury to Broca's area does not harm the ability to understand speech, since that is performed mainly by Wernicke's area, in the upper part of the temporal lobe. Wernicke's area is responsible for understanding words as well as producing coherent language and passing on information to Broca's area. If Wernicke's area is damaged, one result is a severe loss in the ability to understand speech. Although a patient can still speak fluently, he tends to talk nonsense. This condition is known as receptive, or comprehension, aphasia.

Language and Communication

The development of language was perhaps the single greatest leap in the formation of the human mind. It allows man to pass on knowledge from one generation to the next, and people to communicate complex ideas precisely both by speech and written symbols.

All language is made up of elements arranged at several different levels. At the lowest level are the individual sound units, the phonemes. At the next level are morphemes – a group of phonemes that have some meaning but are not complete words. Examples are the "ed" in walked, which makes the verb past tense, or the "es" in glasses, which indicates the noun is plural. The next level is that of whole words, which can be of several types. Each type performs a different role in the sentence. Nouns indicate objects or people, and verbs indicate actions or states of being. Above this level are groups of words called phrases. The sentence "The boy kicked the ball" can be broken into a noun phrase "The boy" and a verb phrase "kicked the ball". The verb phrase can be broken down further into the verb "kicked" and another noun phrase, "the ball".

The understanding of language has advanced greatly since the 1950s, largely because of the ideas of an

HIEROGLYPH EGYPT	SOUND VALUE	MEANING	HIERATIC EGYPT	PHOENICIAN 1300 B.C.	GREEK 500 B.C.	ROMAN 100 A.D.
	k	vessel				K
	n	water				M
	ch	serpent				N
	r	mouth				P
	k,g	pot				C
	sh	field				S
	ari	eye				O
	tep	head				R
	l,r	lion				L

The chart above gives a few examples of how early Egyptians came to represent sounds by a kind of picture writing called hieroglyphs. Their technique gradually evolved and other scripts and alphabets developed from it.

International symbols, shown right, were devised to help people find important facilities in countries whose languages they may not understand. These symbols from an international sign language for airports and rail stations easily cross language frontiers and show (1) station restaurant, (2) medical facility, (3) this way to buses, (4) electric power source, (5) stop warning, (6) telephone, (7) male and female.

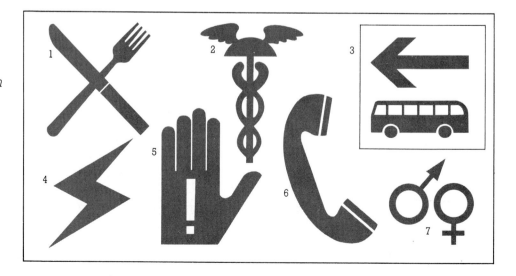

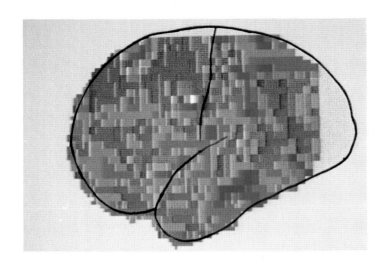

The brain areas involved in reading silently are shown here in red. They are similar to those used in reading aloud, but the auditory cortex of the temporal lobe is not involved.

American linguist, Noam Chomsky. He realized that all languages are governed by rules that are unconsciously present in the mind of any speaker. He set out to discover what these rules are and invented a test to check if proposed grammatical rules are correct. If they are, they must be able to generate all possible grammatical sentences within a language and not generate any ungrammatical ones. Rules of language are so difficult to formulate, however, that despite much effort no complete set has yet been worked out to account fully for the grammar of any one language.

Chomsky also presented the idea that sentences have deep and surface structures. Some sentences may appear the same on the surface but because they arise from different deep structures, they have different meanings. "They are cooking apples" could tell us either that people are preparing fruit with heat, or that the fruit is suitable only for cooking, not for eating raw. Other sentences may be different on the surface but have the same deep structure. "I read the book" and "The book was read by me" appear to be different sentences but, because they arise from the same deep structure, the reader or listener knows they mean the same thing. To understand the meaning of a sentence, the listener must unconsciously analyze its structure and also know the meanings of the words in it. The interplay between the structure of language and the meanings of individual words within it gives language its flexibility.

Children use the rules of grammar effortlessly by the age of ten. By then their sentences contain complicated noun and verb phrases. Psychologists suggest that there are three ways in which a child acquires the use of language. First, a child may learn by imitation, and this is the only way individual words can be learned. Second, a child unconsciously guesses the underlying rules of language and then tests the guesses. As the child matures, he learns there are exceptions and refinements to the rules he has discovered. A third way to acquire language is to learn by instruction. Studies have shown, however, that most parents give children no formal language instruction. Many psychologists believe that there may be inbuilt mechanisms in the brain that enable the growing child unconsciously to discover from what it hears the underlying rules of grammar, but no one has yet succeeded in discovering what these mechanisms are.

The Kalahari Bushman storyteller, below, has a trained memory that is a repository of his tribe's history and wisdom. In a society without a written language, he is the library.

Brain and Body

The human nervous system has two distinct parts. One is the central nervous system – the brain and spinal cord – which contains most of the body's neurons. The other part is the peripheral nervous system – the motor and sensory neurons, and the neurons that convey information to and from the spinal cord and brain. The peripheral nervous system is subdivided into the autonomic and somatic systems. The autonomic system governs the internal organs and monitors breathing, heart beat and digestion. A person has little conscious control over the autonomic nervous system.. The somatic system transmits messages from external stimulation of the skin as well as from muscles and joints, and controls the muscles of the skeleton. The motor pathways in the somatic system are subject to conscious control.

All nerves of the peripheral nervous system contain bundled axons, which are usually insulated from each other by a special membrane, called a myelin sheath. This sheath stops their signals from interfering with one another and speeds up the transmission of nerve impulses. Each nerve has two branches, one for each side of the body. The twelve nerves serving the face and throat are the only ones to enter the brain directly, without passing through the spinal cord. They include the optic nerves, which carry information from the eyes, the auditory nerves running from the ears, and the trigeminal nerve, which conveys information from the skin of the face, the mouth and the teeth, and the nasal cavity.

Thirty-one pairs of nerves communicate between the spinal cord and the rest of the body. They all contain axons transmitting information from the senses and axons controlling the muscles. At the spinal cord each nerve divides so that the axons of the neurons carrying

The neural pathways in the body, shown at right, are nerve bundles connecting sensory, motor and glandular activity to the central nervous system. Except for the cranial nerves, which enter the brain directly, each section is named after the region where it enters or leaves the spinal cord.

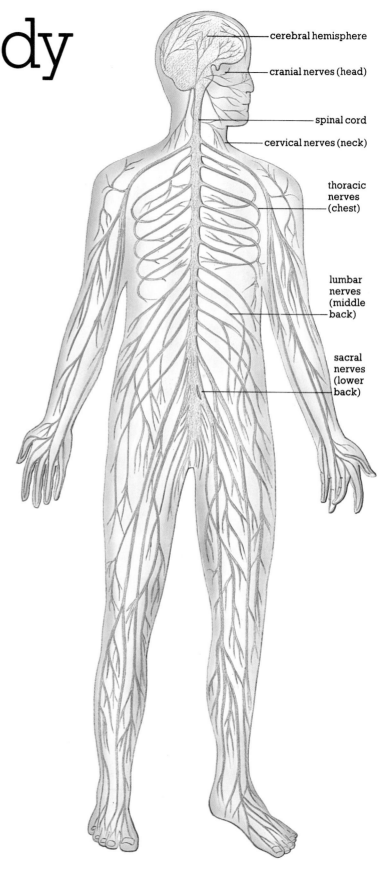

cerebral hemisphere

cranial nerves (head)

spinal cord

cervical nerves (neck)

thoracic nerves (chest)

lumbar nerves (middle back)

sacral nerves (lower back)

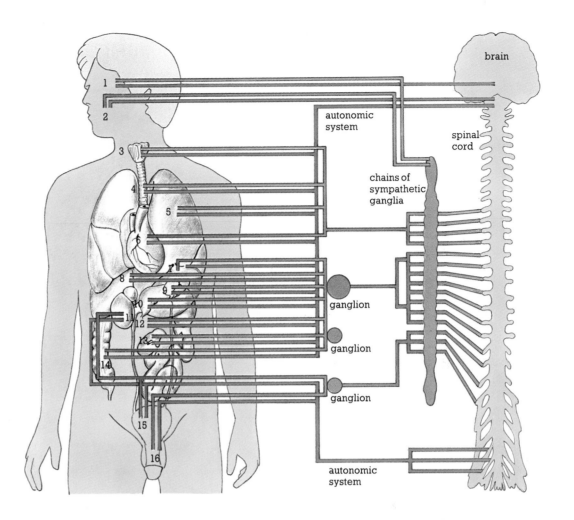

sympathetic fibers
parasympathetic fibers

1 eye   2 salivary glands
3 larynx   4 trachea
5 lung   6 heart
7 stomach   8 liver
9 adrenals   10 pancreas
11 kidney   12 blood vessel
13 small intestine   14 large intestine
15 bladder   16 penis

The autonomic nervous system, at right, controls the glands and other internal organs. Its divisions – sympathetic and parasympathetic – gear the body for activity, then restore balance afterwards. The state of the body at any moment is the result of the interplay of their influences. Ganglia are clusters of cell bodies within the peripheral nervous system.

sensory information (the sensory neurons) enter the rear of the spinal cord, and those controlling the muscles (the motor neurons) leave from the front. The matter of the spinal cord itself is continuous with the brain and contains many synapses.

Much of human muscle activity is coordinated by the spinal cord, and most muscles work in pairs, one to flex open a contracted joint, the other to extend it. The motor neurons have synapses in the spinal cord that inhibit each other in order to prevent damage caused by pulling a joint in opposite directions. Some simple actions are directly controlled by the spinal cord. For example, when a person stubs a toe and pulls his foot away without thinking, it is because some of the sensory neuron terminals in the toes make contact with motor neurons that cause the thigh muscles to flex. This direct link gives us rapid protection from injury, since the message does not have to go to the brain and then return to the foot through the spinal cord. Such re-

actions are called spinal reflexes and take place in many of the muscles of the trunk and limbs.

The autonomic system governs the glands and internal organs through two subdivisions, the sympathetic and parasympathetic. These subdivisions tend to operate in opposite ways. When people are aroused, the sympathetic division prepares them for violent action. Heart rate is increased, and extra blood is sent to the muscles. The liver releases into the blood glucose, a sugar that fuels the muscles. The hair stands up and the sweat glands begin to work so that extra heat can be lost quickly. The parasympathetic division reverses these effects and restores and conserves energy. Blood is diverted from the muscles to the digestive tract. The secretion of saliva and digestive juices then help to absorb food and restore energy levels. The delicate balance between the two divisions of the autonomic system is vital to the proper functioning of the internal organs.

Biological Drives

For the maintenance of life, the internal state of the body must be kept within certain limits and this balance is called homeostasis. The mechanisms regulating these limits are known as biolgical drives, and people are born with them. These drives insure that body temperature remains constant, that blood and tissues contain the right amount of water and that a person takes in enough food to provide energy. The centers regulating these drives are located in the hypothalamus and the limbic system and are governed by special receptors.

Within the hypothalamus are cells that monitor the temperature of the blood circulating there. If the blood is too cold, the cells cause shivering to generate heat from the motion of the muscles. They also reduce heat loss by constricting blood flow through the tiny blood vessels near the surface of the skin. If the blood is too hot, heat is lost by erecting the body hair and by sweating. The amount of water in the body is controlled by receptors in the kidneys. They detect the volume of water in the blood while other receptors in the hypothalamus monitor its salt content. If there is too little water, or if the blood is too salty, water is absorbed from the kidneys into the blood stream. A person will then feel thirsty and begin to drink. As it takes about twenty minutes after drinking begins for the additional water to be absorbed into the blood, far too much water would be taken if drinking continued until the balance in the blood were correct. The amount of water being drunk is measured by receptors in the mouth and

The limbic system, below, lies in the space between the cerebral hemispheres touching the surface of the forebrain. The structures are interconnected with each other and the cortex by many different routes. The larger scale drawing on the right shows the components of the system.

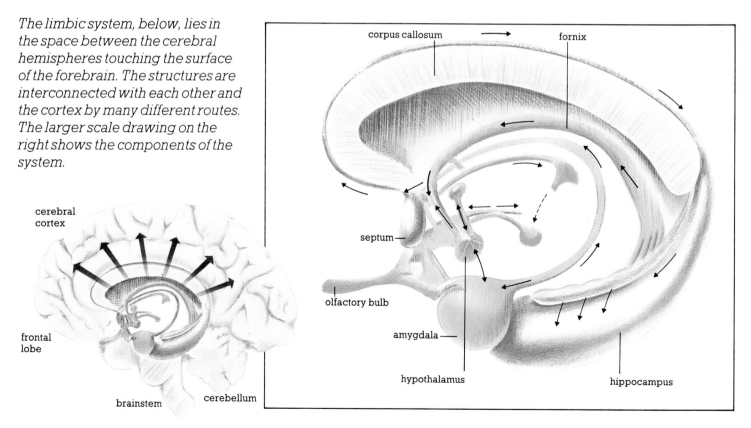

corpus callosum   fornix

septum

olfactory bulb

amygdala

hypothalamus

hippocampus

cerebral cortex

frontal lobe

brainstem   cerebellum

Many other factors affect hunger and the type of food people like. Both when and what they eat are partly the result of habit and social convention.

Reproduction is also a biological drive, but it exists for the survival of the species rather than the individual. How this drive develops and how it is regulated is extremely complex. Sexual development does not begin until a fetus is about six weeks old. Then, under control of the genes, the testes or ovaries begin to develop. They secrete the male and female sex hormones. These hormones largely regulate the further growth of the sexual organs, although their activity is monitored by other hormones from the pituitary gland, which is itself controlled by the hypothalamus. In most animals, the presence of sex hormones at a critical stage, usually soon after birth, determines whether the animal develops male or female patterns of behavior. In people learning and habit also seem to play a part in determining both the nature of human sexual identity and the frequency of sexual activity. The ways in which people give expression to their sexual drive depend heavily on the customs of their societies, as do the roles that men and women traditionally play within those societies.

This thermograph, a picture that is made using heat rather than light to produce images on film, shows a couple kissing. White areas are the hottest, as indicated on the scale. Sex is an example of behavior that combines both instincts and learning.

The graph below shows the stages an animal or person would go through when recovering from an injury to the area of the hypothalamus that controls food intake. As the injury heals a more normal pattern of solid food and liquid consumption is established.

throat. They signal that thirst is satisfied when enough water has been drunk to make up the deficit in the blood.

Eating is largely controlled by receptors sensitive to the level of blood sugar. The areas of the brain that regulate feeding appear to use several neurotransmitters, especially serotonin. Doctors have used this discovery to help people who are obese. Drugs that raise the level of serotonin or epinephrine switch off the neurons that signal hunger. These "off" signals may be specific to particular foods. Serotonin appears to switch off hunger for sugar but does not affect consumption of protein. It is also involved in triggering sleep, and the sleepiness that follows a good meal may reflect the increase of serotonin because of the intake of sugar. Serotonin may also play some part in insuring that people feel hungry at particular times of the day.

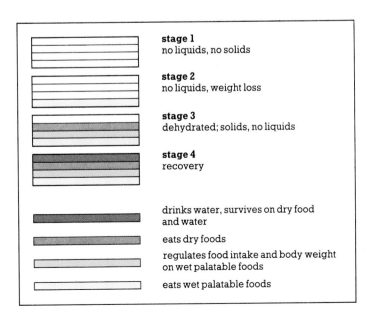

stage 1
no liquids, no solids

stage 2
no liquids, weight loss

stage 3
dehydrated; solids, no liquids

stage 4
recovery

drinks water, survives on dry food and water

eats dry foods

regulates food intake and body weight on wet palatable foods

eats wet palatable foods

Emotions

Emotions are strong feelings that determine how we tend to act. Love, hate, anger, grief, frustration, guilt and fear are all emotions. Emotions are accompanied by physiological arousal of the autonomic system. Most emotions are reactions to our dealings with other people. Some, for example, sexual desire or maternal love, are based on biological drives. Although there is arousal in hunger and thirst, they are not counted as emotions, perhaps because they are not related to other people.

Many different emotions are accompanied by strikingly similar bodily reactions, called emotional arousal. Such arousal is caused by the hypothalamus and other parts of the limbic system activating the sympathetic division of the autonomic nervous system. Nerve impulses from the limbic system go to structures in the brainstem and, in addition, the hormone epinephrine is released into the bloodstream in conjunction with nerve impulses from the limbic system and the hypothalamus. As a result important changes take place within the body that gear people to action. These physiological changes are usually called the fight-or-flight reaction.

In the nineteenth century two psychologists, William James and Carl Lange, suggested that what people feel depends on what they do, not the other way around. For example, people feel angry because they strike someone, or they feel afraid because they run away. James and Lange said that people first react to an environmental change and this reaction unconsciously produces emotional arousal. This theory was strongly criticized and an alternative, known as the Cannon-Bard theory, was formulated. It states that the experience of the external world and the physiological response occur at the same time. The thalamus integrates stimuli from the environment and simultaneously sends messages to the cortex, which labels the emotion, and to the autonomic system, which produces physiological arousal. Under different circumstances, each theory can appear to be correct. When people are in sudden danger, rapid action often seems to come before the feeling of fear – that is, the bodily arousal (James-Lange), but at other times people are consciously aware of an emotion but may have no need or opportunity for action (Cannon-Bard).

Another theory, developed in the 1960s, drew together information about what happens in the brain and body during emotional arousal with data on how people interpret their feelings and evaluate them by using information stored in memory. This theory states that feedback to the brain from organs activated by the autonomic system causes people to have a generally heightened arousal. Which emotion we say we experience depends on how we interpret our state This means that emotions that last far longer than a fight-or-flight reaction are subtle combinations of conscious thought and physiological arousal. It is likely that emotional experience is caused both by the activiation of the sympathetic division of the autonomic nervous system and by the way people interpret events in the light of their motives.

Injuries to the nervous system can alter the way people feel and express emotions. When people have damage towards the top of the spinal cord, the link between physical arousal and conscious interpretation is severed. They still experience different emotions, but less intensely. Damage to the amygdala, a small body in the limbic system, may make animals excessively placid. In a few cases of pathological aggression in human beings, surgeons have attempted a cure by removing the amygdala. Since the limbic system has connections to the frontal lobes, damage to these lobes can make people apathetic and lacking in emotion. Epilepsy centered in the temporal lobes sometimes makes people very excitable. There is even evidence that such epilepsy can produce feelings of ecstasy and religious awe.

The physical expression of different emotions, for example grief and hysterical excitement, shown here by mourners at a funeral (right) and fans at a pop concert (far right), can be remarkably similar. The label given to the internal feeling relies on a mix of conscious interpretation of physiological changes and environmental factors.

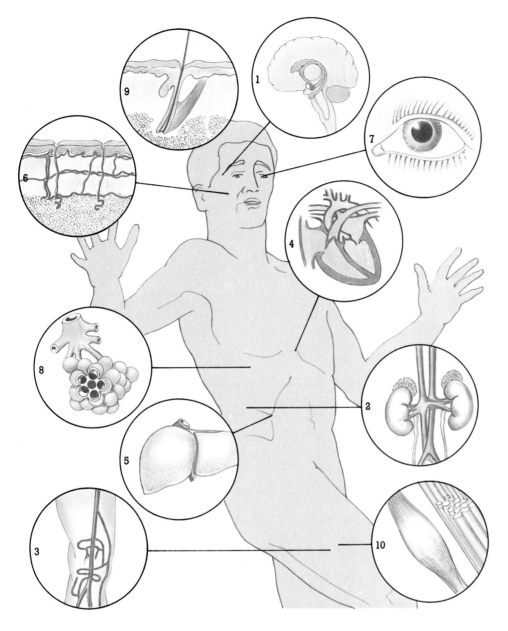

The diagram of the fight-or-flight reaction on the left gives some idea of the many bodily processes that are activated by strong emotional stimuli. (1) The pituitary gland (red) secretes hormones into the system, (2) the adrenal glands (yellow) above the kidneys secrete adrenalin, (3) large blood vessels dilate to speed blood flow, (4) heart rate and blood pressure rise, (5) liver releases glucose for energy to the muscles, (6) blood vessels near the skin contract, (7) pupils of the eye dilate, (8) air sacs of the lungs expand, (9) hair stands on end, (10) muscle tension increases.

Pain and Placebo

The sensation of pain acts as a warning of, and is usually caused by, actual or impending damage to the tissues of the body. The physical events that cause pain may occur at the surface of the body, for example in the skin or teeth, or in organs deep inside the body. Pain can be produced by sharp pressure, extremes of heat and cold, or irritation of tissue caused by harmful chemicals. Almost everyone experiences pain. A few individuals are born without the ability to feel pain. But they are not as fortunate as one might think, because they are unaware of injuries and illnesses that damage their bodies.

Some receptors in the skin are specialized for signaling pain, though it is likely that other receptors also play a role. Pain signals take a special pathway in the spinal cord to the relay center of the brain, the thalamus, and from there to the somatosensory cortex, where the sensation is registered. They also run to the RAS, which when active produces alertness. The frontal lobes, which receive signals from the limbic system, play a part in determining how much distress pain causes. Scientists do not know the exact role the cortex plays in pain, but it can determine how unpleasant a painful event seems. Soldiers in battle can suffer severe injuries but report that they feel no pain until they arrive at a dressing station. Ignoring pain in this way is part of the human ability to pay selective attention to what is happening.

Morphine, a drug extracted from opium, greatly reduces pain. Recently scientists have discovered that there are neurotransmitters in the brain, endorphins and enkephalins, that act like morphine on the nervous system. They bind to the same receptor sites as morphine. If the neurons containing these neurotransmitters are stimulated by an electric current, they release the transmitter and reduce pain. Another chemical, Substance P, appears to be the main neurotransmitter responsible for transmitting pain signals up the spinal cord. Morphine is a highly addictive drug

In the diagram below, pain messages from an injury pass to the somatosensory cortex and the reticular activating system. In the first circle, these messages, using Substance P, pass across synapses in the spinal cord. Enkephalin regulates the degree of pain felt by blocking the messages conducted by Substance P. In the second circle, a higher degree of magnification shows how this blocking occurs.

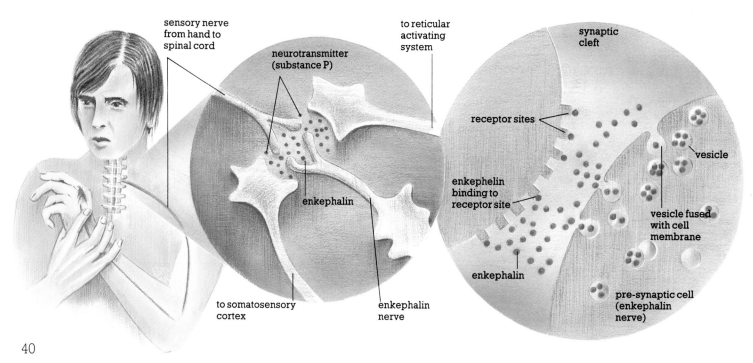

sensory nerve from hand to spinal cord

neurotransmitter (substance P)

enkephalin

to somatosensory cortex

enkephalin nerve

to reticular activating system

synaptic cleft

receptor sites

enkephelin binding to receptor site

enkephalin

vesicle

vesicle fused with cell membrane

pre-synaptic cell (enkephalin nerve)

and although it is an excellent pain killer, if given repeatedly it is necessary to increase the dosage. It has been found that the dosage needed for terminally ill patients levels out, and they can survive for months on a high dosage. Morphine supresses many of the body's vital functions, such as breathing. In the hope that endorphins and enkephalins will prove to be less addictive than morphine and have fewer dangerous side-effects, drug companies are spending much time and effort on experimenting with these substances.

Although pain is largely determined by the physiology of the brain, clearly psychological factors are also important. One aspect of the psychology of pain is called the placebo effect. A patient given a placebo, a dummy pill made of sugar, and told it is a strong pain killer often feels less pain. Experiments suggest that because the patient expects the pill to help, his body secretes more enkephalin, for example and it reduces the pain. Acupuncture, an ancient Chinese technique of inserting fine needles into certain places in the body in order to relieve pain elsewhere, may also work through the release of enkephalins. Whether the success of acupuncture is due to the needles or the placebo effect is not yet known. Even though psychological factors affect pain, they do so by influencing the nervous system. Thus, the synapses, in the parts of the brain that control emotion – the limbic system and the hypothalamus – use endorphins and enkephalins as neurotransmitters.

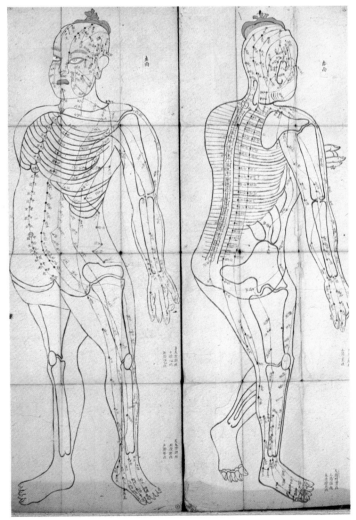

The painting of a festival, above right, shows a charlatan selling elixirs, marvelous liquids for the relief of various disorders. For centuries these were in common use. Some were herbal remedies that contained healing substances, others were no more than flavored or colored water or could be poisonous. When these potions cured, they did so by the power of suggestion, acting as a placebo.

This Chinese chart on the right shows the sites where acupuncture needles are inserted. It is used in training for qualification as an acupuncturist. Acupuncture is currently undergoing close scientific investigation.

Stress and Anxiety

Some experience of stress and anxiety is normal, even in people leading healthy, fruitful lives. Mild stress even produces alertness and interest, but how people deal with stress depends on many factors. The physiological reactions to stress, which are part of the fight-or-flight reaction of the sympathetic division of the autonomic nervous system, can become too extreme or inappropriate to the situation, and then problems arise. Prolonged stress and anxiety may lead to physical illness. If a person regularly eats hasty, unhealthy meals because of pressure at work and at home, constant indigestion may be succeeded by the acute pain of a bleeding stomach ulcer.

Moderate levels of anxiety can, however, actually be beneficial, for example, in the positive way stress works when a student takes an examination, a situation most students find stressful. Parents, teachers and friends tell students how important the examination is, and that their future may depend on the result. If in response to this stress, a student has no anxiety, then he could be too casual and not make enough effort. Being overanxious would also damage his performance. He would spend time worrying about the physical symptoms of his anxiety – an upset stomach, increased sweating, shakiness. Irrational fears could buzz in the mind: how will I remember everything? Are these trick questions? Is this all too much for me? Experiments suggest that having just the right amount of anxiety in a stressful situation is the way to perform well. It motivates one to prepare carefully, to be quick but not careless, to answer the right questions or perform the right actions and to pace one's work so there is no last minute panic. Different levels of stress produce the best performance in different tasks. In general, the more difficult the task, the lower the level of stress needed for best performance.

The immediate physiological reactions to anxiety prepare people for violent activity, the fight-or-flight reactions. These reactions were probably essential in the distant past when early man frequently needed to resort to violent physical exertion in order to survive, especially in a difficult or hostile environment. Today

Children taking tests in the classroom have very individual responses to the stress stimuli. Controlling these is important to achieve the best performance.

The people in the photographs above are subject to stress. When people consume food quickly in noisy and distracting surroundings, as above, stress can cause digestive problems. The faces of the people in the photograph above right show different reactions to the pressures of the New York subway at rush hour. Commuters who face crowded and unpleasant conditions every day need to achieve a certain degree of mental control to cope with the stress to which they are subjected.

The chart on the right shows how a person's oxygen consumption, an indicator of stress level, drops in a slow and gradual curve as he falls asleep. It also shows the far greater and immediate drop that can be achieved if the person has been trained to produce the relaxation response when under stress.

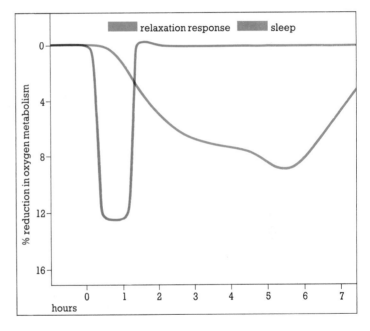

most problems are solved by decisions that require careful thought rather than by direct physical exertion. Thus the levels of anxiety people experience often are too high for what they are doing. The prolonged presence in the blood of the hormone epinephrine, which is involved in the fight-or-flight reaction, can cause severe damage to the heart and circulatory system and to other organs. Violent physical activity reduces the amount of this hormone in the blood. Someone driving a car for a long time in heavy traffic is under constant stress, but since he is not physically active, the epinephrine level in his blood remains too high.

People can learn to cope with stress. The most obvious method is to exercise, avoid being overweight and avoid too much alcohol and other drugs. In addition it is possible to learn how to relax both body and mind, and there are techniques that teach people how to cope with events without becoming too worried or upset by them. People can be taught to adopt a more confident and serene attitude to life and to reduce the negative feelings associated with stress. Knowledge gained from animal experiments and new treatment techniques for people suggest that stress will be less severe if people can control the outcome of a stressful situation.

Psychosomatic Illness

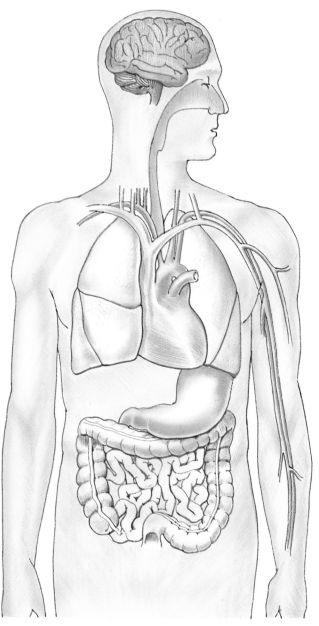

A psychosomatic illness is a physical disorder produced or aggravated by someone's psychological condition or by his behavior. The behavior may include such habits as overeating, smoking, drinking too much alcohol or taking too little exercise. There is a clear link between such behavior and the development of a variety of physical illnesses. Other physical illnesses are produced by more subtle psychological factors. A patient's mental attitude, personality, level of stress, life style and even life events such as marriage, bereavement, promotion or unemployment may contribute to, or even initiate, a disorder.

Among the diseases that can be psychosomatic are those that make breathing difficult (bronchial asthma), raise blood pressure (essential hypertension), and irritate the skin (eczema and neurodermatitis), the stomach (peptic ulcers) or the bowel (ulcerative colitis). All are probably related to harmful changes in the functioning of the autonomic nervous system. Trying to understand the psychological as well as the physical problems involved gives medical science a better chance to devise successful treatments.

When people are under stress the sympathetic division of the autonomic system gears the body for action.

Psychosomatic disorders can affect many parts of the body, but the six illustrated are particularly vulnerable. (1) Many types of headaches can be caused by anxiety and muscle tension. (2) Influenza is a virus infection, but susceptibility and recovery are affected by the patient's mental state. (3) Asthma frequently worsens under stress. (4) Lifestyle can contribute to heart disease, especially high blood pressure. (5) Stomach acidity is affected by mental attitudes and the environment in which food is eaten. Too much acid erodes the stomach's protective lining. (6) Ulcerative colitis develops similarly to stomach ulcers. (7) Skin rashes can occur anywhere but the inner surface of the joints is especially vulnerable.

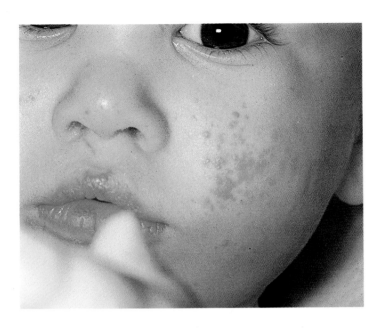

This child has a skin inflamation called eczema. Eczema may be an allergic reaction in many cases but once contracted it often recurs in times of emotional distress or need.

A person might remark "my adrenalin was really flowing," and this would be literally true. Should this happen too often, or too continuously over a long period of time, the organs affected by autonomic arousal may be damaged. Although scientists do not yet know precisely how stress makes some people more likely to develop physical illnesses, some links are clear. For example, under psychological stress, the brain alters the amount of hormones secreted into the blood by the endocrine glands, particularly the pituitary and the adrenals. Prolonged changes in hormone levels not only damage some organs but they also affect the body's immune system, which protects it from invasion by infections. There is evidence that the high levels of arousal that occur under prolonged stress can cause narrowing and blocking of the arteries.

Trying to discover if certain personality types are particularly vulnerable to specific illnesses is very complex, but a few clues have been found. Scientists know that life style and significant life events make people more vulnerable to disease. Individuals who have what is called a "Type A" personality drive themselves hard. These people are usually overcommitted to their work, strive intensely after achievement and are highly competitive, aggressive and impatient. They have an extreme sense of urgency, even when there is no need to hurry. It is possible that these traits make people vulnerable to heart disease, but their behavior and other inborn factors that operate on the brain and the circulatory system may also be significant. Recent research suggests that it is not so much hard work that predisposes people to heart attacks as hard work done without achieving satisfaction. Other studies have shown that after what are called major life events, such as the loss of a spouse or bankruptcy, people are at special risk. Death, even excluding suicide, is three times more likely than usual after such an event. Surprisingly, sometimes even major positive changes, marriage or promotion, for example, cause vulnerability too.

A highly speculative suggestion is that even the growth of cancer cells may be influenced by stress. There is evidence that influenza or the common cold is more likely in time of stress. This supports the view that psychological factors affect not only the autonomic system but the immune system as well.

The painting below was submitted by a female entrant to a competition for migraine sufferers. The painting was done from memory to depict how she felt during an attack and illustrates her distress.

Biofeedback

It used to be believed that change in blood pressure or heart rate could not be brought under conscious control. Then in the late 1960s a series of ingenious experiments devised by Neal Miller and Leo DiCara, two American psychologists, tested this assumption. Laboratory rats were given the drug curare to ensure that their heart rate could not be influenced by movement or muscle tension in the skeletal muscles. Because of the effects of the drug, the rats were put on artificial respiration machines. Only direct control over the autonomic nervous system, and thus the heart muscle itself, could change the heart rate. The experimenters then tried to teach the rats that if they increased their heart rate when a light came on, they would receive a small electrical current to one of the brain's pleasure centers, in this instance in the hypothalamus. It is well known that animals will work for such a reward. The result of the experiment startled the scientific community. The rats did learn to increase (or decrease) their heart rates in response to signals. There has been considerable debate about these results and no one has succeeded in repeating the

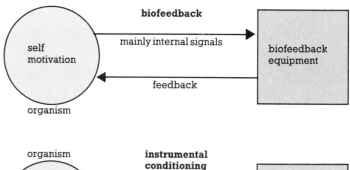

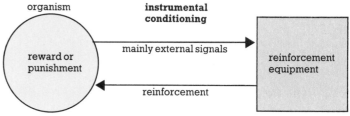

The similarity between the mechanism for biofeedback and instrumental learning is shown above. In humans, although aspects of learning and reward are important, other factors, such as what the patient thinks about the procedure and its benefits, also affect performance of the task.

In teaching the use of biofeedback to control muscle tension or brain wave type, a first session may be conducted in a group setting such as this. Research has shown that if the subjects are allowed to play with the apparatus before serious learning takes place, then learning will take place more quickly.

experiments. Today many other involuntary responses have been investigated in people as well as laboratory animals.

These experiments gave rise to a new technique known as biofeedback, which has shown that some control over involuntary functions can be exerted, at least by some people. The word biofeedback is short for biological feedback. It means that information about a bodily system – for example, blood pressure – is measured by instruments and then fed back to the person by some external route. Information about people's involuntary responses is collected, usually by electronic sensors on the skin, amplified and turned into a signal that can be easily understood, for example a variable tone or a series of bleeps. There are other more sophisticated ways of delivering the feedback. A computer-run television screen can show physiological changes as a graphic display or by differences in color and light intensity. If blood pressure is to be brought under control, then the normal blood pressure of someone at rest might be shown as a horizontal line in the center of the screen. Changes in blood pressure are shown as a contrasting line moving up and down as blood pressure increases or decreases. The task is to make the line drop to the normal level. Since it is known that performance depends on reward, it might be asked what reward someone receives for making the

display move nearer to the target. Psychologists believe that for people to discover they can carry out the task is ample reward. In addition, if someone has high blood pressure, he knows that success will bring better health and general well-being. The only disorder where biofeedback seems to be genuinely helpful is tension headaches. The patient sees the level of muscle tension displayed as a line on a screen and tries to reduce the height of this line. Once he has learned to relax the muscles of his head and neck using biofeedback, he usually finds that he can do it in his ordinary environment. For most disorders, the changes people can make are too small to be of much medical use. Scientists are unclear how patients succeed in gaining conscious control but the feedback display may help them to identify the response that brings about physiological change and allow them to repeat it. It is possible that with improved techniques of biofeedback, it may in the future be useful for treating problems, such as epilepsy and the recovery of control over the muscles after a stroke.

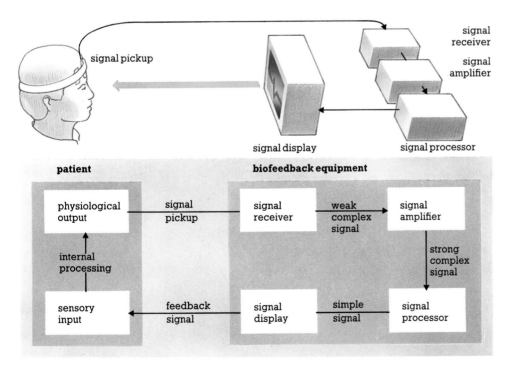

The schematic diagram on the left shows the main components of a biofeedback system that might be used in a health clinic to treat a variety of stress disorders.

Conditioning

Inborn involuntary responses are called unconditioned reflexes and they happen automatically. For example, the eye blinks when a puff of air hits it. The blink protects it from possible damage. An event detected by the sense organs, whether registered consciously or unconsciously, is called a stimulus (the plural is stimuli). In this example, the blink of the eye is an unconditioned response (UCR) to an unconditioned stimulus (UCS), the puff of air.

The famous Russian physiologist Ivan Pavlov (1849-1936) discovered that it was possible to train animals to make an unconditioned response to new stimuli. He showed that if each time a bell sounded food were given to a dog, after several trials the dog would salivate at the sound of the bell before the food was given. The stimulus to which a new response is formed – in this case the bell – is called a conditioned stimulus (CS). When the unconditioned response – in this case salivation – is given to the conditioned stimulus, it is called a conditioned response (CR).

The UCR to sudden pain is to withdraw the affected part of the body. If whenever a bell is sounded, it is

A baby just a few hours old demonstrates that the eye blink is a true unconditioned response. A monitor has been painlessly fixed to its head and a dedvice on the sheet of plastic registers each blink produced when a tiny puff of air from the tube above the head provides the stimulus.

Ivan Pavlov (near right) is seen in his laboratory with colleagues and one of the dogs used in his pioneering conditioning experiments. The chief motivation behind Pavlov's objective and repeatable study of complex mental processes was the belief that they could be a vital clue to the workings of the nervous system.

A ballet dancer, far left, will usually adopt a recognizable version of one of the classic positions of the feet, even when relaxing at home. Years of instruction and practice have conditioned her to turn her feet out in this way. Sneezing, left, is an unconditioned response and is not learned. It is usually caused by irritation of the sensitive membrane of the nasal cavity. It is such a powerful reaction that it is very hard to control.

followed by an electric shock to the hand, people soon start to withdraw their hand at the sound of the bell even if they are unable to avoid the shock. Once this CR is learned, people may find it difficult to resist moving their hand at the sound of the bell, even if they are told it will no longer be followed by a shock. Many emotional responses may be learned in this way. Fear can easily be conditioned to previously neutral stimuli, and it can be conditioned to some stimuli more readily than to others. For example, fear in people is readily conditioned to small animals that move quickly – such as mice – and to snakes and to spiders. It is possible that in the past this type of fear helped man's survival. This type of learning is called classical conditioning. Because of its simplicity it is easy to study, particularly in animals.

The CR, once acquired, is not easily lost. Months after the initial learning period, an animal that has been conditioned will still make the CR when the CS is given. Pavlov also discovered that it is possible to learn not to make a CR. He first trained dogs to salivate to a bell and then sounded the bell repeatedly without giving food. The dogs salivated less and less to the sound of the bell on its own and eventually ceased to salivate at all. This procedure is called extinction. Even after extinction, however, some traces of the CR may remain. If a new learning period is introduced, the subject usually

relearns the CR in fewer trials than were required to learn it originally.

A response learned to one stimulus can also be triggered by similar stimuli, a process called generalization. For example, if two stimuli such as similar tones are sounded, one always followed by an unconditioned stimulus, such as an electric shock, and the other never, at first the subject responds to both. In time, however, the subject ceases to respond to the stimulus that is never followed by the UCS but continues to respond to the one that is, a process known as discrimination. The survival value of generalization and discrimination is obvious. Two similar stimuli are usually followed by the same consequences, but sometimes they mean something different, and people and animals must be able to learn to tell them apart.

It has become apparent that conditioning is more complicated than was once thought. For example, if an animal is conditioned to a particular conditioned stimulus, say a light, and then another stimulus, say a bell, is added, the animal does not condition the response to the second stimulus.

Learning and Reward

A process known as instrumental learning was identified by the American Edward Thorndike (1874-1949), and later investigated by other psychologists, most notably the American B.F. Skinner. It was discovered that animals will learn to make new responses to obtain rewards or to avoid punishments. In a typical animal experiment, a rat is put in a cage containing a lever. While exploring the cage, the rat usually presses the lever by accident and then receives a food pellet. A hungry rat quickly discovers the link between lever and food, and it will press the lever repeatedly. The food, a form of reward, is said to reinforce the behavior of lever pressing. Almost any response can be reinforced by a reward that satisfies one of the animal's biological drives. Such rewards are primary reinforcers, and this type of instrumental learning is called positive reinforcement. A secondary reinforcer is something that has previously been associated with a primary reinforcer, or can be used to obtain one. Secondary reinforcers, such as money, are useful in the instrumental conditioning of people.

Instrumental learning can also be used to teach people or animals to avoid some unpleasant stimulus, which is known as a negative reinforcement. For example, a rat will quickly learn to jump a hurdle in its cage at the sound of a bell to avoid receiving an electric shock.

Many of the principles of classical conditioning apply equally to instrumental learning. Remove reinforcement and the response will gradually be lost, but if the reinforcer is introduced again, the behavior is usually relearned more quickly than when it was first acquired.

For reinforcement to modify behavior, people and animals must detect that it has occurred. They must also store in their brains the events that preceded the

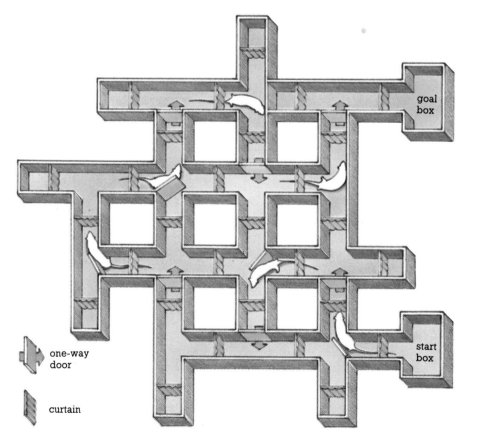

one-way door

curtain

goal box

start box

Instrumental learning has been the butt of many jokes. Above, one rat says "Boy, have I got this guy conditioned. Every time I press the lever, he drops in food."

A maze learning task, such as the one shown on the left, tests an animal's ability to learn from trial and error. Even without reinforcement, a rat finds its way by developing a mental map based on exploration.

reinforcement. There are areas in the limbic system that yield a sense of pleasure when stimulated and it is likely that they detect reinforcement. Two nerve pathways starting in the midbrain and ending in the limbic system and cortex are probably active in registering reinforcement. One uses the neurotransmitter norepinephrine, and there is some evidence that it is involved in primary reinforcement. The other pathway uses the neurotransmitter dopamine and may be involved in governing which goals are sought at a given time.

Despite the importance of reinforcement, it is also clear that not all learning depends on reinforcement. Learning can also take place by observing other people, a process called modeling. For example, children may learn sex-role behavior from identifying with the same sex parent. It is likely that children's tendency to model their behavior on their parents is to some extent inborn, but reinforcement may still play some part. To become like someone one admires is a kind of reward in itself. Experiments have shown that adults tend to model themselves on people who most resemble them. If someone sees the model rewarded for certain behavior, this also enhances learning. Similarly, people learn many things merely out of curiosity or simply through being exposed to them. This kind of learning, called latent learning, was clearly demonstrated by experiments in the 1930s.

The pigeon above is learning to discriminate. It is rewarded for pecking one pattern but not the other and thus is learning to link the correct pattern with reinforcement.

Playing a one-armed bandit is kept interesting by a carefully planned reinforcement rate. When reinforcement-winning occurs at irregular intervals, there is a stronger tendency to continue than if reinforcement were given at every attempt.

Motivation

People have many motives beyond fulfilling their biological needs. Curiosity, the wish to be liked, the search for fame or fortune, the need to succeed and find fulfilment all develop to a different degree in everyone. Most of these motives are learned and are not directly related to physical needs, although some motives clearly derive from biological necessity. For many people earning money is a means to an end that is purely biological; they need money to obtain food and shelter. Sometimes the secondary reinforcer, money – which can be exchanged for a primary need, food – becomes a motivating force itself. Millionaires, who initially may have wished to make money for the comfort and security it brings, often become engrossed in making more and more money for its own sake. All the activities related to making money reinforce the initial drive. When this situation occurs, psychologists say that the learned drive has become "autonomous".

Curiosity is almost certainly an inborn drive, which all mammals display. A rat placed in a new environment will explore it systematically. Monkeys will learn to press a lever repeatedly if they can obtain a view of a room or a slide of a scene that interests them. Curiosity also has obvious survival value. Animals must learn to find their way around their environment. They must learn the safe places to which to flee in time of danger, and also places where supplies of food and water may be found. A great deal of human behavior is motivated by curiosity.

In man certain types of motivation are thought to develop out of the way a child reacts to parental praise. A child learns that certain behavior brings approval. In time, the child takes over the parent's role and begins to think "I did that well, didn't I?" Many social psychologists believe that this pattern underlies most learned motivation. Gradually people develop internal standards of behavior, and reaching that standard becomes a reward in itself. Failure causes either a resetting of

The triumphant expression of a championship runner as he wins his race shows that intense striving for athletic achievement is rewarding. The competitive urge is easily learned and culturally conditioned in most Western technological societies.

A father's attitudes and behavior toward his child have been shown to be particularly important in experiments investigating achievement motivation. Children with high need achievement will have been encouraged more by their fathers.

There are great similarities in the behavior patterns of people who create vast industrial and financial empires. They begin by struggling against obstacles and become more concerned with power as they succeed. The men shown on the left exemplify this pattern. Henry Ford (top) initiated the assembly line as a means of increasing the speed of production of his automobiles. Aristotle Onassis (center) began to build a shipping network when the Greek economy was depressed in the 1920s. Alfred Krupp (bottom) employed new techniques to reconstruct the ruined German steel industry after the end of World War II.

the standard or greater efforts to reach it.

The following experiment shows this type of motivation at work. Watched by their parents and an investigator, a group of ten-year-old boys was asked to build a tower using irregularly shaped bricks. Parents of boys previously judged high in the need to achieve gave more praise than did those of the boys with low achievement needs. The fathers of the high need-achievers were more friendly and less domineering. They did not give specific advice to their sons, only hints. Part of learning the need to achieve is learning to use one's own judgment. There is evidence too, that if parents set impossibly high standards, a child may give up. Fear of failure becomes so great that it inhibits performance.

The way parents give praise may also play a part in the way sex role behavior develops. In many societies, boys are rewarded for exploring their environment and for being dominant, girls for being submissive and caring. Experiments show this can happen even with babies a few days old. Parents playing with girls dressed as boys tended to reward male-type behavior, which led to increased behavior of this type. Learning by observation is also significant. As a child watches others being rewarded, it learns to predict the consequences of its own actions. This type of learning plays an important part in the formation of adult personality.

Personality

Personality is the mixture of mental, emotional and behavioral traits that characterize an individual. Psychologists have attempted to devise objective classifications of personality using techniques such as direct observation, questionnaires, interviews and projective tests. Each method has its strengths and weaknesses. When completing a questionnaire, a person may be frank or merely say what he or she thinks is expected. Asked to describe a friend, colleagues may know how a person responds only in one set of circumstances. Trained interviewers may have preconceived ideas and therefore may not observe an important facet of someone's personality. A projective test – one in .which a person looks at pictures and says what ideas or thoughts they arouse – is not always reliable either. These tests are based on the idea that people will unconsciously project their own emotions into the pictures. Unfortunately, the results may be interpreted in different ways and they may vary from one day to the next.

When a large number of personality traits are

This is one of the ten main symmetrical inkblots used in the famous Rorschach test. Based on the Freudian view of personality, the Rorschach is a projective test that has been used extensively since the 1930s in an effort to discover aspects of personality, fantasies and psychological state.

In this picture a student is giving her reaction to an image from the Thematic Aperception Test. Such tests direct people to "project" their own emotions into the picture by simply asking them what is happening. This can be a useful way of discovering aspects of the personality that people might otherwise be reluctant, or find impossible, to disclose.

measured by questionnaire, it is usually found that there are groups of traits on which a person tends to get roughly the same score. Within such a cluster, someone who rates high on one trait will rate high on the others. By putting together all the traits in such a group, psychologists try to describe broad characteristics that can then be used to divide people into personality types. One such important division is known as introversion-extroversion. The introvert tends to be quiet, reserved, careful, thoughtful, pessimistic and rather unsociable. The extrovert is sociable, outgoing, talkative, impulsive and optimistic.

One of the problems in measuring personality is that the same person may exhibit a trait in one situation but not in others. Personality may change over time as well. One investigation assessed personality traits in the same people at the age of sixteen and then at thirty-six. Only one trait in three showed any tendency to remain constant. Inheritance, too, plays a considerable role. Personality has been shown to depend on the state of the central nervous system, and the fact that introverts can be conditioned more easily than extroverts suggests that this distinction has a biological basis. Damage to the brain, particularly to the limbic system, can alter personality radically.

Since the 1950s studies by American psychologists

The children of an Amazonian Indian tribe, above, are conditioned from an early age to behave in stereotypical male or female ways. Boys are schooled in aggressive behavior, such as hunting; here they have caught a huge snake. Girls learn submissive and domestic tasks, such as making pots.

have produced evidence about the way experience combines with inborn personality. Babies seem to have three distinct temperaments: easy, difficult and slow to warm up. The easy baby is regular, adaptable, and likes being approached. The difficult baby is quite the opposite, while the slow to warm up baby has a mildly negative attitude to approach and adapts slowly to new stimuli. Easy and difficult babies are similar to the extrovert and introvert types while the slow to warm up, like so many of us, is somewhere in the middle. Provided a baby is born into a family that takes account of its inborn style, all will be well. In one study undertaken in a hospital in San Francisco it was found that day-old babies of Chinese descent were much more peaceful and less fretful than occidental babies. None of the babies had been handled by their mothers. Generally, most psychologists think that personality is the result of the combination of inborn traits and their molding by experience.

Measuring Intelligence

Intelligence is the capacity to learn and think effectively. In the past people assumed it to be a general ability, distinct from memory or the capacity to acquire new knowledge. Some scientists have wondered if general intelligence really exists or if it is just the sum of distinct mental skills. Research shows that people who do well on one type of problem generally do well on others. This supports the general intelligence theory, but special abilities are also significant. It is possible that how well a person performs on a specific kind of task depends on the development of the area of the brain that carries out the task. In general, women do better at verbal tasks than men, while men do better at spatial tasks, and there is some evidence that the brain's language centers develop earlier in women. Sometimes testing reveals a specific difficulty, which could be the result of a learning problem or, rarely, brain damage.

Intelligence tests contain a variety of questions grouped together in sub-tests, each of which measures a mental skill. Some may ask what is the deliberate error in a picture or how to assemble a geometric jigsaw puzzle. Word games and problems are common,

The five problems at the bottom of these pages are similar to those used in IQ tests. The problems measure abilities that are highly related to general intelligence. (The answers appear at the bottom of the opposite page.)

The child shown above is trying to fit a variety of shaped objects into matching holes. This kind of intelligence test for preschool children does not depend on verbal skills or prior learning, and may form part of a longer test.

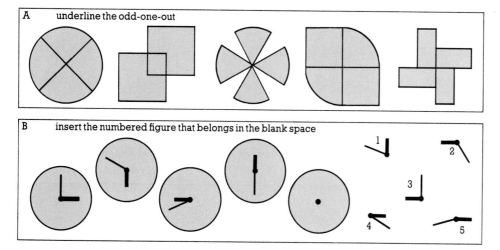

A underline the odd-one-out

B insert the numbered figure that belongs in the blank space

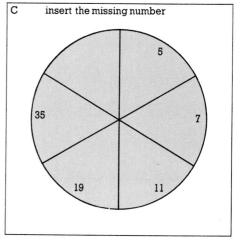

C insert the missing number

35   5   7   19   11

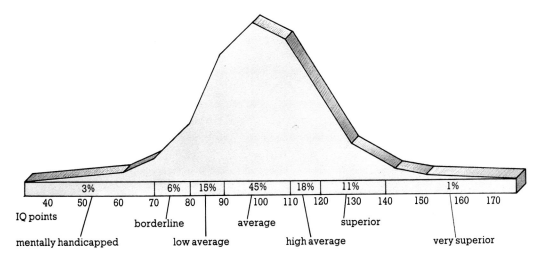

This percentage profile of IQ distribution is taken from the Stanford-Binet Intelligence Test. Forty-six percent of the population have scores between 90 and 110. The shape of the graph is called the normal distribution.

and so are questions in mental arithmetic. The test designers try to avoid items that require special knowledge but they usually do assume some basic level of education. To test children or adults who have had no schooling, they devise tests that rely chiefly on visual material. To cope with people from different societies that have different views on what is a commonsense approach to a problem, "culture fair" tests have been created. They too rely mainly on visual items.

When a test is being constructed, individual items are tried out on a large number of people. Generally the results of most items correspond well with each other. For example, if many people fail a difficult question, it will be answered correctly only by those achieving high scores over all the questions. If the results from an individual question do not relate consistently to those from other questions, then it is eliminated from the overall test. When a reliable bank of test questions is created, the test is standardized by being tried out on another large group of people. In choosing the group, the test designers try to reflect accurately the class and racial groups in the society that will use the test. Finally, all scores are listed in order from lowest to highest, and the score exactly halfway up the list is arbitrarily called 100, the average. The score is the intelligence quotient (IQ). A score twenty-five per cent higher in the list is assigned 110 and twenty-five per cent lower, 90. In practice most people score between 70 and 130. Calculating scores in this way measures a person's performance in relation to other people, not against some abstract standard.

An IQ score can give a moderately good prediction of education performance, but many other factors, such as motivation to study and personal attitudes, are vital. IQ tests measure only some aspects of what people casually call intelligence. We do not yet know how IQ relates to personal insight, the ability to make friends or to be artistically creative.

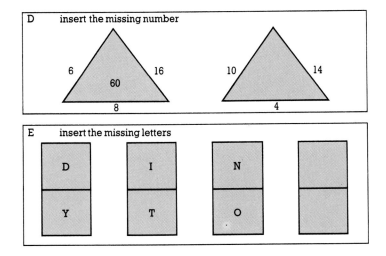

(Answers: A – Drawing 2. B – Number 4. The minute hand goes back ten, the hour hand goes forward three. C – 67. Clockwise, each number is the preceding one multiplied by two minus three; an alternative explanation is that clockwise, each number has had twice the amount added to it as the preceding one. D – 56. Multiply each number outside the triangle by 2 then add. E – The fifth letter forward is S; the fifth letter backwards is J.)

Is Intelligence Inherited?

Intelligence tests measure a person's current ability to reason and also predict possible future intellectual performance. Psychologists, teachers and parents often want to know whether intelligence is inherited or acquired through experience. Psychologists have tried to find out how much each factor contributes to overall intelligence, but without much agreement being reached.

Different kinds of upbringing give children more or less experience in the kinds of reasoning being measured by intelligence tests. Practice can raise someone's IQ by as much as ten points. Research also shows that differences in the testing environment can affect performance. In African countries, children who go to school score more highly than those who do not. To answer IQ questions correctly, a child or adult must understand that the test is a kind of game. If they have no experience of playing with ideas in this way, their scores will be lower. Research demonstrates that people from primitive tribes have difficulty in answering the sort of abstract questions set in tests. If a question says, "All houseowners pay tax. Boima is a houseowner. Does Boima pay tax?" an African child may reply, "No, he doesn't. The government let him off because he is the tax collector." The child understands the connection between taxpaying and houseownership but, not being used to the game, relates the question to his own experience.

From a biological point of view, research with rats indicates that the brain may change in response to different environments. Some rats were put in ordinary cages while others had an "enriched environment," cages with toys and many different activities. When the mature rats were killed and their brains weighed, those from the enriched environment had slightly heavier brains. This suggests that varied experience plays a role in the physical development of the brain, and hence of intelligence. Nevertheless the post-mortem study of the brains of men of genius has failed to reveal any differences from other human brains.

There is also considerable evidence that inheritance plays an important part in determining intelligence. Strong evidence comes from the study of adopted children who had been separated from their natural parents at an early age. When their IQs were measured, they corresponded more closely to the IQs of their natural parents than to their adoptive ones by whom they were brought up. Since the brain is a biological organ, it is hardly surprising that intelligence is, at least in part, inherited.

Facts about the inheritance of intelligence must be examined carefully because it is not yet possible to make precise comparison with the role of environment. If everyone had exactly the same genetic makeup then all differences would be due to environment. In fact,

The diagram below shows the difference between using two-dimensional tests for pattern matching. Both tests measure the same ability. However, children in a Nigerian village did poorly on the task in two dimensions but as well as children in other societies when using three-dimensional objects, with which they were more familiar.

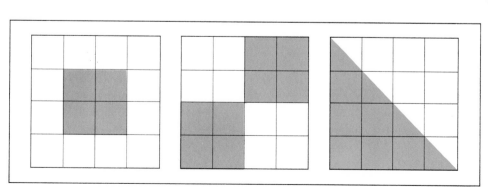

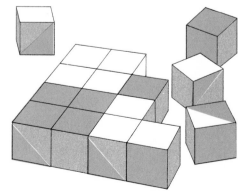

This graph shows the combined results of many studies that looked at the degree of similarity in IQ scores between children and their biological and adoptive parents. There is a close correlation between children and their biological parents even when the children were brought up by adoptive parents. This contrasts sharply with the low relationship between the children and their adoptive parents.

although identical twins tend to be much more similar in intelligence than a pair of people chosen at random, they still exhibit some differences. Even though inheritance plays a part in determining IQ, a good environment at a very early age may improve intelligence. Environment enrichment programs in the United States have attempted to provide a more intellectually stimulating setting for underprivileged children before they go to school. These succeeded in raising the children's average IQ, but often it dropped back when the program stopped. Perhaps this was because the programs were not followed through long enough and did not involve the parents as well, particularly the mothers.

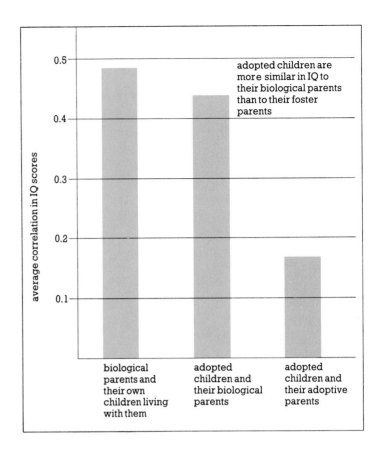

adopted children are more similar in IQ to their biological parents than to their foster parents

average correlation in IQ scores

biological parents and their own children living with them

adopted children and their biological parents

adopted children and their adoptive parents

Irene and Jeanette are identical twins who were separated at six weeks of age. Thirty-three years later they were re-united and although they were brought up in different environments, they have amazingly similar tastes and aptitudes. Their lives have many parallels but the oddest is that Jeanette has a wasted muscle in her hip but never feels the pain and Irene has pain but no muscle damage. There is only a one point difference in their IQ scores.

How We Think

Daydreaming, wishing, inventing fantasies, toying with new ideas, reading, writing, planning, making decisions, working out problems – all are different forms of thinking. These are examples of conscious thought, but we must remember that conscious thought is determined by other processes that are simultaneously going on in our minds. Psychologists distinguish two kinds of thought – undirected and directed. Undirected thinking has no clear objective; directed thinking always has a specific purpose.

From studies of undirected thinking, psychologists have learned that daydreams and fantasies are influenced by our physiological state, by external events and by conscious and unconscious wishes. The sight of something we cannot afford may trigger daydreams of being rich. The biological significance of daydreams and fantasies is unclear, but one theory is that they are a way of allowing drives to discharge themselves harmlessly.

More is known about directed thinking and it is divided into two types, deductive and inductive reasoning. When we think deductively, we follow a

In the test of deduction above the subject is asked if a card with a vowel always has an even number on the reverse. To find out, the subject can turn over two cards only. People often fail because they look for evidence to support the theory rather than disprove it. Turning over a vowel and an odd number would check the idea accurately. The sort of mistakes made on this kind of task are called errors of inference.

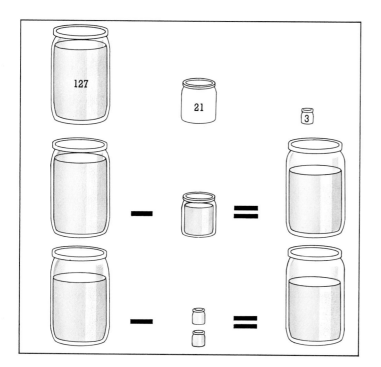

The problem in inductive reasoning, left, asks you to discover the rules by which the problem shown here can be solved. Three jars hold 127, 21, and 3 quarts respectively. You must measure 100 quarts. By working backwards from the solution you will find the method that applies to this problem, which is shown in three stages starting at the top.

series of steps that we know will produce a solution to a problem. We apply a general principle to a particular situation. An example of deductive thinking would be to use arithmetical rules to work out a budget. Often, however, we deduce something not by using rules but in a more indirect way, using visualization to help. If we are told "Mary is more clever than Jane and Jane is more clever than Sally" and then asked "Who is more clever, Mary or Sally?", we may construct a visual image with the most clever girl, Mary, at the top and the others ranked below her. Then we read off their relative positions from our visual image.

We use inductive thinking when we need to discover a method to solve a problem. We start now, not with a general rule, but with the facts at hand. Many methods of problem solving are discovered by trial and error, often using an approximate solution, analyzing the difference between it and a target solution, then progressively reducing the difference. We acquire the best methods of strategies by practice. A wide repertoire of strategies does not guarantee successful problem solving, but it makes it more likely and quicker. Chess players learn many strategies, some of which are unconscious. Flexibility in strategy selection is also important and may be associated with the work of the brain's frontal lobes. A person with brain damage there often finds it difficult to switch from one strategy to another.

Perhaps the best known explanation of how thinking develops is that of the Swiss psychologist, Jean Piaget (1896-1979). Although his ideas have influenced much educational practice, many psychologists do not fully accept them. Piaget thought the child goes through several logical stages in learning how to think. In the first two years, infants learn to coordinate actions with environmental stimuli. By the end of this stage the infant has learned that objects have a permanent existence. If something disappears behind a screen, the child knows that it is still there. Gradually the child learns to build a model of the world in its mind and over the next eight years learns to use this model more accurately. A four-year-old child does not understand that when water is poured from a tall, thin container into a short, fat one, the amount of water does not change. He thinks there is more liquid in a tall, thin glass than the short, fat one. By the age of ten or eleven, the child understands that the amount remains the same. Over this period children also become less egocentric. They learn to see the world not just from their own point of view, but from that of others. Abstract thought is mastered only after a child reaches the age of ten or eleven. During this period children start to reflect on their own thought processes and come to appreciate such things as formal logic.

Studies of daydreams reveal several common patterns. Relaxing scenes such as the exotic beach, left, are often elicited in response to the question "Think of something relaxing." Other themes involve the wish to achieve something, or a fantasy of identification, such as wanting to be someone else or to be like someone else.

The Creative Mind

Creativity is the ability to produce original and appropriate ideas. Originality alone is not enough. Clearly one element of creativity is an inventive way of looking at the world. A second element can be called heightened perception, the recognition of significant aspects of people, things and situations that others miss. Ultimately, persistence is needed to apply ideas and carry through plans. Most people are creative only in one or a few related fields. There are creative artists, poets, novelists, scientists, inventors, football players and businessmen, but no one is creative in all these spheres. This suggests that one has to master the techniques of a particular art or science before it is possible to be creative in it.

Because certain problems cannot be solved by the application of known rules, they need a new or creative idea for their solution. The British psychologist Edward de Bono has devised tests for the skill he calls lateral thinking, an important part of creativity. The production of new ideas by lateral, or divergent, thinking contrasts with convergent thinking, in which a solution is reached by using already known rules. In practice, divergent thinking for new ideas and convergent thinking to check their feasibility must be combined. Here is a lateral thinking problem. You are put in a room with two strings hanging from the ceiling and a wrench lying on a desk. You must join the two strings without removing them from the ceiling, but they are so far apart you cannot reach them at the same time. The solution is to tie the wrench to one of the strings and swing it like a pendulum. You can then catch it, while holding the other string. To solve the problem you had to have a new idea, realizing you can make a pendulum by tying the wrench to one of the strings. Having arrived at this idea by divergent thinking, you must check that it will work by convergent thought, which is more routine. Are the strings close enough together for you to catch the swinging one while still holding the other?

Attempts have been made to develop tests for divergent thinking, or creativity. An open-ended question is given, such as how many uses can you think of for a brick? One ten-year-old boy answered "to make buildings with or smash a shop window in a robbery." Another, obviously more inventive, suggested "Bricks at ten paces, turn and throw. No dodging allowed," a suggestion for a brick duel. This type of test tries to measure how easily new ideas are produced. Other tests investigate word skills and flexibility in dealing with geometric patterns. In this type, higher scores are achieved for unusual answers. If asked to name as many round things as possible within a short time, obvious answers such as buttons or plates score for

Here is part of the result of one kind of creativity test. The task was to use a square in as many ways as possible. In these tests each item produced is scored. The eight items drawn here are ordinary ones changed to fit the test requirements.

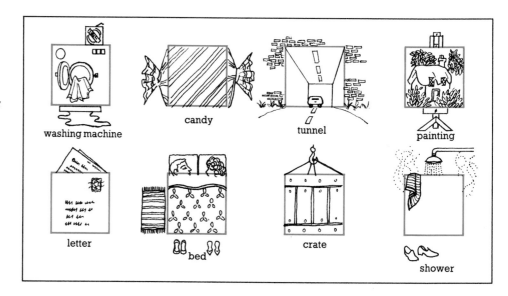

washing machine

candy

tunnel

painting

letter

bed

crate

shower

The drawings on the left by Leonardo da Vinci (1452-1519) are outstanding examples of creativity in both art and science. The top drawing shows horse-propelled scythes that could be used in war or agriculture. The bottom drawing shows an idea for a tank that could be propelled by a horse or a man. Both designs show a balance of creative and practical thought.

quantity only, while unique answers such as mouse-holes are scored for originality. In practice, creativity tests have been disappointing since different tests give different results and none of them seems to predict genuine creativity.

It is possible that creativity requires a certain level of intelligence, but once that level is reached, other factors become more important. There is evidence that highly creative people usually do well on standard intelligence tests. One study found that creative people tend to be idealistic, energetic, independent, self-assertive and versatile. Similarities in their up-bringing show that learning is important too. On the negative side, creative people can be discontented, disturb any organization to which they belong, have a tendency to find fault in others, and be stubborn and temperamental. Although creativity is a subject that fascinates many scientists, of all the processes of the mind, it remains one of the most mysterious.

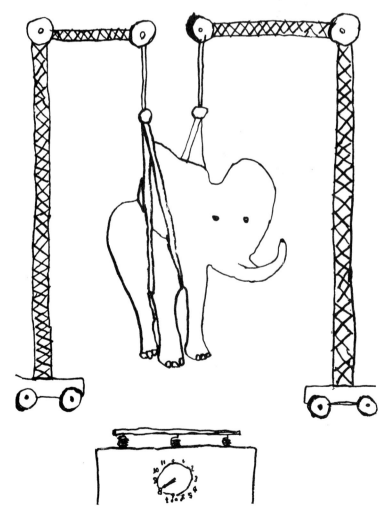

This drawing shows one seven-year-old boy's idea for weighing an elephant. Analyzing the techniques used by children in problem solving gives clues to the nature of creative thinking. Edward De Bono, has pioneered studies of this kind of "lateral" thinking. The child has allowed both for the animal's weight and its physical safety. The elephant is slung from two cranes and balanced on giant spring scales.

Memory

Psychologists think that there are three kinds of memory, each of a different duration. The shortest is sensory memory, of which one example is iconic memory, in which visual stimuli are preserved for fractions of a second. If a display of numbers arranged in rows is flashed up and then, immediately after the numbers disappear, a pointer is set to one of the rows, the observer can read out the numbers that were there. This means that all the numbers must be available for recall for a brief time – about half a second – after they disappear. Iconic memory is important in visual perception because it smooths the transition between one image and another. There is a similar memory related to hearing.

A second kind of memory, called short-term memory, depends on keeping material continuously in consciousness. If a telephone number is read and then repeated over and over in the mind, it is possible to dial the number without rereading it. By rehearsing a number in this way you can remember it for as long as your patience lasts. As soon as you start to think of something else, the number is usually lost. This is sometimes called working memory, because it consists of material

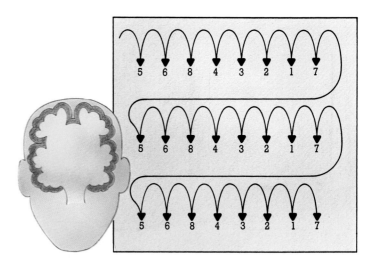

Experiments have shown that there is an upper limit of about eight pieces of information for the rehearsal loop of short-term memory.

with which the mind is currently working. It roughly corresponds to consciousness.

The third kind of memory is long-term. Although material may have to be rehearsed to enter long-term memory, once stored it is retained for long periods without further rehearsal. With sufficient practice, a ten-digit number may be retained for hours, weeks or even years without ever being called back to consciousness for rehearsal. Most of the items in long-term memory are more significant than mere strings of numbers. For example, individuals store information about people they have met, things they have learned and many experiences they have had.

There are several theories about how information is stored in memory. One is that in short-term memory a number of neural circuits in the brain become active and continue to be active as long as a person thinks about the material. Long-term memory must involve more permanent change. One possibility is that whenever one neuron fires another, there is an increase in the tendency of the first cell to fire the second, thus

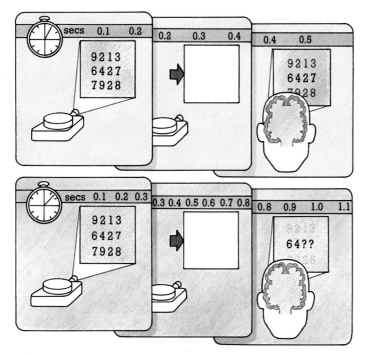

The diagram, left, shows the stages in an iconic memory experiment. The most important factor is the time lapse between seeing the image and the presentation of the pointer directing you to recall it. A gap of as little as 0.4 of a second reduces the content of iconic memory enormously.

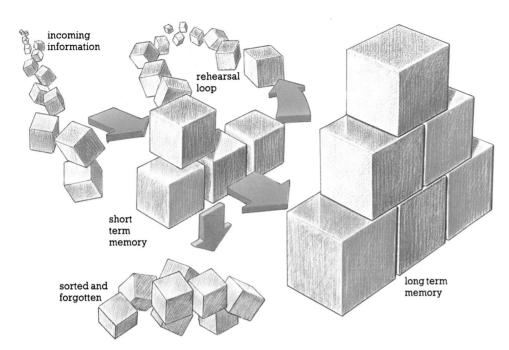

incoming
information

rehearsal
loop

short
term
memory

sorted and
forgotten

long term
memory

Sorting and rehearsal, both shown left, are factors in how the mind decides what should be passed into long term storage. Much information that a person assumes forgotten can be recalled under unusual circumstances, such as hypnosis. Forgetting is just as necessary as remembering; otherwise memory would be overloaded with trivia.

creating a new pathway in the brain. There is, unfortunately, no direct proof of this theory. Whatever the nature of the new connections underlying long-term memory, they seem to take some time to become established. Some scientists think memory is localized, especially in the temporal lobes, and it is true that people who suffer brain injuries to the temporal lobes generally have memory problems. However, research suggests that many other parts of the brain are also involved in memory storage.

The hippocampus may have a role in selecting what should go into long-term memory, but other processes are at work in causing people to forget. For example, synaptic changes that occur when new circuits are formed may, in time, simply revert back to their original state. A new memory may be blocked if the brain already holds a very similar one. Known as the "interference theory," this explains why unique skills such as swimming and driving are rarely forgotten while similar skills, as squash and tennis players know, often conflict. Another theory says that people forget not because the memory is gone, but because it cannot be found. Experiments have suggested that electrical stimulation of temporal lobes may cause people to remember things they assumed to be long forgotten. As this research has been carried out on epileptics, however, scientists do not know if the results apply to normal brains.

In complex tasks, such as flying this Boeing 747 aircraft and reading the flight deck information display, all aspects of memory are required. Long term memory provides basic skills, short term is used for individual flight observation, and iconic for moment to moment smoothing of the rapidly changing visual stimuli. The designers of flight decks and other information displays must understand and allow for many features of memory and perception when they create their designs. The science of tailoring equipment to the physical and mental capabilities of man is called ergonomics.

Altered States of Consciousness

Most of conscious experience is concerned with ordinary events. Sometimes people, though still awake, may be either removed mentally from the world around them or may experience the world in a very different way. These altered states of consciousness can be achieved either through practicing certain techniques, such as meditation, or by taking drugs that affect the biochemistry of the brain.

Many Eastern societies practice some form of meditation. In an elementary form, a person learns to sit comfortably, sometimes with closed eyes, and to relax either by dwelling on each group of muscles in turn and letting them go loose, or by repeating a single powerful word – a mantra – in time to slow and regular breathing. In some other varieties of meditation the meditator focuses his attention on a particular object, which may be a physical object – a flower, a vase – or a

concept such as unity or god, and tries to go into a state of total absorption or heightened awareness. In Zen, a Japanese variety of Buddhism, the meditator lets his thoughts flow passively while observing them. Gradually, he becomes increasingly emotionally detached until he reaches the state of having no sense of involvement – pure detachment. Anyone who tries can learn some form of meditation.

Taking drugs to alter consciousness can be extremely dangerous. Opium, a drug produced from the poppy *Papaver somniferum,* and its derivatives morphine and heroin produce a feeling of intense pleasure (a "thrill" or a "rush") within a minute or two of being used. This sensation is succeeded by a period of extreme mental calm in which the user feels he has no unsatisfied needs. These drugs, the opiates, have very similar effects on the brain as the neurotransmitters known as

The Meo tribesman from Laos, on the right, is smoking opium through a traditional pipe designed for this purpose. Smoking opium does not help a person control his mind but produces euphoria. For centuries the drug has also been used to suppress pain.

The Buddhist monk, far right, is sitting in the full lotus position, which is often used by those who are adept at controlling the mind in contemplation.

The Japanese girl on the left is beginning one of the first classic exercises to develop tranquility for meditation. She is gazing steadily into a bowl of clear water. Concentrating on it clears her mind of distractions.

endorphins and enkephalins. Opiates are extremely dangerous because the brain adapts to them and to repeat the initial effect the user finds it necessary to take more and more. If deprived of the drug, the addict feels intolerable sensations of nausea, sweating, abdominal cramps, agitation and insomnia. Amphetamine ("speed") when injected also produces a thrill or "buzz," but this is often followed by extreme irritability, which leads the user to repeat the dose. One of the major effects of amphetamine is to cause the release of norepinephrine, a neurotransmitter found in the pleasure centers of the brain.

Marijuana, or cannabis, produces changes in sensation. Sounds and tastes seem to take on new and unusually pleasant qualities. Time seems to pass very slowly, and the user may become very relaxed and open to new ways of looking at the world. There is some evidence, however, that these effects have to be learned, and that people tend to join in with the general feeling of the group with whom they are taking the drug.

Lysergic acid diethylamide (LSD) is dangerous even in a single dose. The effects of LSD, which is thought to act by blocking the receptor sites in the brain normally occupied by the neurotransmitter serotonin, are highly unpredictable. In some people it causes intense hallucinations of vivid colors and sounds, while in others, it induces what seem to be mystical experiences. It may also cause panic and complete loss of control, and some users have killed themselves while they were under its influence.

Although any of these drugs may produce pleasurable experiences for a time, none of them helps the user to think or act more effectively. In the dosage needed to give pleasure, they cloud consciousness and make it difficult or impossible for the user to think coherently or rationally. It is known that these drugs cause their effects either by imitating the action of neurotransmitters or by altering their activity, but scientists do not know why changes in neurotransmitter activity cause specific changes in mental function.

67

Sleep and Dreaming

Perhaps the least well understood biological drive is that for sleep. A baby sleeps for about sixteen hours a day, adult men average eight hours and women about seven and a half hours. As people grow older they usually need less sleep.

During sleep, the electrical impulses of the brain change dramatically. These brain waves, which are probably caused by large groups of neurons firing in unison, can be recorded on graphs through electrodes placed on the scalp. Scientists discovered that people experience two alternating kinds of sleep, called paradoxical and orthodox, depending on whether or not dreaming is occurring.

The twenty-four-hour cycle of sleep and waking, known as circadian rhythm, is a kind of physiological clock regulated by the pineal gland at the top of the brainstem. This clock synchronizes the body to the day-night cycle of the environment. Once set, it keeps good time. People feel disturbed by "jet lag," because their physiological clock is out of phase with the time zone. It takes about one week for it to reset itself.

As people fall asleep, they move through stages marked by different kinds of brain waves. When a person is awake and alert, the brain waves are fast, irregular and weak (beta type). Just before sleep a regular (alpha) rhythm develops, interspersed with slower (theta) waves. Known as the hypnagogic state of pre-sleep, this is when people often experience strong sensations such as falling, but can still react to important external events because they are not truly asleep. Orthodox sleep begins with Stage I, lasts only a few minutes and fades into Stage II, in which there are bursts of fast brain waves, called sleep spindles, and

The brain wave patterns of Stages I to IV of sleep are shown on the right with those of the pre-sleep hypnagogic period. Throughout the night, the sequence is repeated with gradual slowing of the brain wave pattern during the successive cycles, as shown clearly by the graph lines widening as the waves register more strongly and slowly. At each change there is an interval of REM sleep, when the sleeper has vivid dreams.

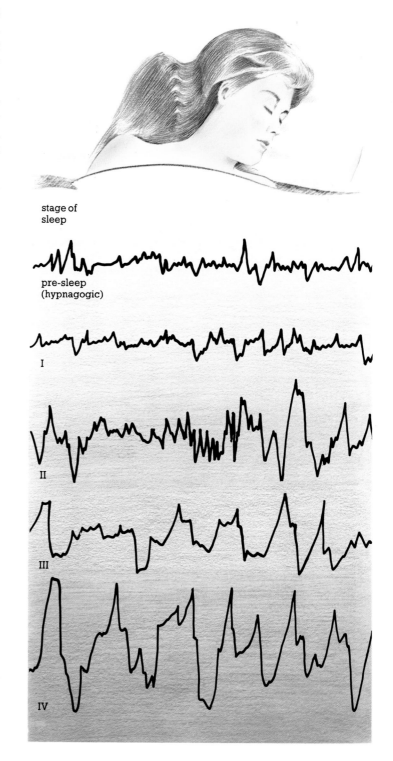

stage of
sleep

pre-sleep
(hypnagogic)

I

II

III

IV

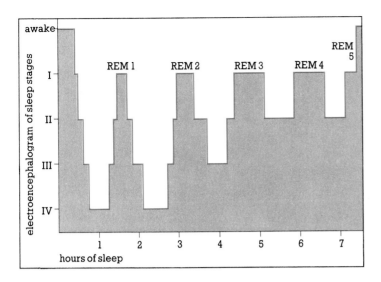

This graph shows the cycle of orthodox (Stages I to IV) and paradoxical (REM) sleep, occurring at regular intervals throughout an average night's sleep. The periods of REM sleep get progressively longer.

some strong slow waves. Now a sleeper may move body and eyes occasionally. After an hour or an hour and a half, Stages III and IV are reached with stronger, slower and more regular waves (delta). But as the sleeper drifts back from IV to III, something strange happens – his brain waves become similar to those produced when he is awake. Breathing becomes irregular and body movements increase. This is paradoxical sleep, so called because although the brain registers alertness, it is difficult to rouse the sleeper. It is also called rapid eye movement, or REM, sleep, because the sleeper's eyes move as though he were watching something. When wakened during REM sleep, which recurs four or five times a night, people report vivid dreams.

Because the cerebral cortex seems to be active and yet is not receiving the usual sensory messages during REM sleep, it may be responsible for dreams. Sometimes external stimuli, the sound of rain for example, are woven into a dream, which suggests that some external monitoring by the brain continues even during sleep. The function of dreams is a mystery, although the most important theory about dreaming

American disc jockey Peter Tripp, right, endured two hundred continuous hours without sleep in 1959. Afterwards he was examined by a team of doctors. One doctor was wearing a tweed suit and Tripp imagined it was made of worms. Such hallucinations are extreme but were caused by prolonged sleep deprivation. Peter Tripp regained his senses after several days' rest.

suggests it is the time when the cortex consolidates the day's learning experience and adds to the memory store. Other theories suggest dreams are outlets for emotional conflict. People awake in the morning refreshed when dreams have "worked," and in fear and confusion immediately after one that has not.

Insomnia, the inability to sleep, is a common complaint, but people often underestimate the amount they sleep. Patients suffering from mania, a severe mental disturbance marked by extreme excitement, sleep very little, while those with depression often wake far too early in the morning. In contrast to insomnia, narcolepsy is a condition that causes a person sometimes to fall asleep suddenly during the day. Insomnia is often caused by anxiety, while narcolepsy may be the result of an imbalance in the brain's metabolism. There is some evidence that underactivity in serotonin synapses produces insomnia in animals, so sleep may be based on a neurosystem using this neurotransmitter. Wakefulness in animals probably depends on a system using norepinephrine, but whether it works similarly in people has not yet been fully confirmed. It is known, however, that anxious or neurotic individuals have high levels of norepinephrine and this may be why they suffer from insomnia.

The Mind in Distress

In both the United States and Britain more hospital beds are occupied by the mentally ill than by people with physical diseases. How people describe the mind in distress gives a clue to the assumptions being made about what is normal and what is not. The phrase "mental illness" implies a medical viewpoint, as doctors think in terms of disease, physical causes and treatments. Mental abnormality suggests disturbed behavior that varies considerably from the accepted social and emotional expressions of a particular society. Mental disorder or disturbance is a broader concept, implying many processes such as personal distress, difficulties with relationships, or unfulfilled intellectual and emotional potential. Mental handicap is different from mental illness. It refers to people whose IQ is so low they cannot lead a normal life.

As with other scientific problems, classification is important so that similar disorders may be grouped together and possible treatments discovered. Psychiatry, the branch of medicine that deals with mental illness, and clinical psychology, an applied science that also studies and treats such disorders, often disagree about classification and treatment. One question often debated is whether mental disorder is really an illness. Some kinds of mental disorder, for example senile dementia, are known to be caused by atrophy of the brain and must therefore be classified as illnesses. Others, such as schizophrenia and manic depressive psychosis, are to a considerable extent inherited and are probably caused by defects in the working of certain neurotransmitters. It would seem reasonable to regard these disorders as illnesses. It is not known whether any malfunction in the brain occurs in neurosis, which may be caused by faulty learning, and it is an open question whether neuroses should be thought of as illnesses.

There are several generally accepted categories for the mind in distress. Brain disorders such as delirium or senility are caused by physical malfunctions and characterized by extreme confusion, and are called organic psychoses. Functional psychoses are severe disturbances in which the patient loses touch with reality and has little or no insight into his condition. Neuroses, another category, usually leave the patient's appreciation of reality intact but the distress experienced is out of proportion to the circumstances.

Personality or character disorders form another category and are difficult to treat. Their symptoms are extreme versions of normal behavior, such as shyness or aggression. Sociopathy is a serious personality disorder. Sociopaths act impulsively, without apparent remorse, are unable to learn from experience or form

The diagram below shows how different types of mental illness are dealt with by using different facilities and treatments. The red cylinders are psychotic problems, the blue, neurotic, and the yellow, personality disorders. Because there are variations in diagnosis and the availability of treatments, many areas overlap. The small dark central core indicates some conditions that are never professionally diagnosed or treated.

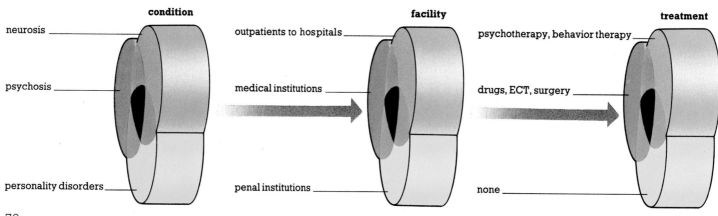

condition
- neurosis
- psychosis
- personality disorders

facility
- outpatients to hospitals
- medical institutions
- penal institutions

treatment
- psychotherapy, behavior therapy
- drugs, ECT, surgery
- none

In the Sudan, and many other parts of Africa as well as Asia, someone suffering from a mental disorder, like the woman in the center of this picture, is considered to be possessed by evil spirits. She is being treated by a witch doctor to restore her to health.

These alcoholics living on the streets of Paris can be thought of as social problems but alcoholism is an addiction and requires understanding treatment and aid.

long-lasting relationships, and may become criminal.

Addictions are a separate group of mental problems, and include alcoholism and drug abuse. Excessive drinking brings about mental and physical damage, and prolonged heavy drinking can cause irreversible brain damage and lead to Korsakov's psychosis, an illness in which long-term memories can no longer be stored. Drug abuse can cause a wide range of harmful physical and mental side effects and be fatal.

Classification depends on observation of the patient and what the patient reports about his or her own state. Treatment for mental illness covers an extraordinary range, from simple advice to the use of powerful drugs or electrical shocks to the brain or, in rare circumstances, surgery. Only a minority of patients need protective and supportive care in an institution and only extreme cases would not survive without it. Although, regrettably, there is still a feeling of disgrace attached to mental disturbance, probably every person has a breaking point, and mental disorders are more common than most people realize.

Psychoses

The psychoses are the most severe form of mental disorder and their symptoms can be very frightening. Although different psychoses have different symptoms, they all involve disintegration of the personality and distortions of thought. When a psychosis is caused by drug damage, poisoning, another illness (such as venereal disease) or the neuron loss that occurs in senile dementia, it is called organic. A psychosis that has no fully understood organic base is called a functional psychosis.

There are two main forms of functional psychosis, schizophrenia and manic-depressive disorder. Schizophrenics often imagine that alien thoughts are being inserted into their minds or that their thoughts are being monitored or broadcast. Frequently they hear, and sometimes see, non-existent things, and suffer paranoia – an overwhelming sense of persecution. They often talk incoherently or become extremely apathetic. Schizophrenia usually starts between the ages of eighteen and thirty-five. One type appears to be triggered by a crisis, while another, which is more difficult to treat, develops more slowly over many years.

Manic-depressive psychosis has two forms. In unipolar manic depression, patients suffer long periods of intense depression, broken by spells of normality. In the bipolar, or cyclical, type, patients fluctuate, usually over a period of several months, between extreme depression and hypomania, a state in which they are continuously overexcited, extremely talkative and

The patient in this photograph is a victim of schizophrenia, a mental disorder that may cause a person to withdraw completely from all social contact. The patient may at first behave in a childlike and irrational manner but later becomes silent and completely immobile. This patient has assumed a characteristic posture like an unborn fetus.

The mysterious figure below was painted by a schizophrenic patient. Many patients show their mental state more clearly in pictures than in words. Here we see a naked figure running across a bleak and threatening landscape.

wildly optimistic. Hypomania sounds enjoyable but can be dangerous. For example, a patient may spend money on things he does not need and be too excited to settle down to any form of work. In the depressive stage, a patient is unable to concentrate, feels worthless, can obtain no pleasure from anything he does and is frequently suicidal.

The physical basis of both schizophrenia and manic-depressive psychosis are thought to be abnormalities in the activity of certain neurotransmitters. One theory suggests that over-activity in the synapses using the transmitter dopamine is a cause of schizophrenia. Drugs that are effective in treating schizophrenia are known to reduce the activity of dopamine, chiefly by blocking its receptor sites on the post-synaptic neuron. The same drugs also tend to produce muscular rigidity and tremor, the symptoms of Parkinson's disease, which is thought to be caused by too little activity in dopamine synapses in parts of the brain's outgoing motor pathways. Heavy doses of amphetamine, which is known to increase dopamine activity, can produce the same symptoms as schizophrenia, including hallucinations and paranoia.

The depressive phase of manic depression may be caused by too little activity in synapses using norepinephrine. The drugs used to treat depression cause

The painting above of crows over a cornfield was painted by Vincent Van Gogh in the last stages of his mental breakdown. The colors are intense and violent and the paint surface thick and turbulent. A few days after completing the picture, the artist shot himself after saying he was going out to shoot crows in the same field.

an increase in the activity of this neurotransmitter. When there is too much or too little of a given neurotransmitter, the brain tends to correct it, so it is possible that the manic phase is caused by an overshoot in the correcting mechanism. Manic depression occurs later in life than schizophrenia and, like it, appears to have an inherited factor, although inheritance may not be the sole cause. Identical twins, particularly those separated at birth, show the importance of inheritance in both illnesses. If one of a pair of identical twins has schizophrenia, the illness develops in the other in only about fifty per cent of the cases. Even after these psychoses have developed, patients can be helped if they live in a supportive and non-stressful environment. About one person in a hundred becomes schizophrenic and a rather larger number suffer from manic depression.

Neuroses

Neuroses are the most common form of mental disorder. The sufferer has great difficulty in coping with life. The neuroses include depression, anxiety states, phobias, hysterical reactions and obsessive-compulsive behavior. Depression accounts for three-quarters of the sufferers. Some disorders, such as anxiety states, affect men and women equally, while others, particularly depression, afflict far more women than men. All statistics on neuroses, like those on other mental disorders, reflect only a small percentage of the people who have them because statistics count only people who come forward for treatment. Many more, prisoners of their own misery, do not.

Neurotic depression is similar to, but less severe than, psychotic depression. Similar biochemical changes probably occur in both, and they can usually be treated by the same drugs. Some viral infections, such as influenza, are often followed by mild depression, presumably because the virus causes changes in the neurotransmitter systems affecting mood. The symptoms of depression include very negative feelings about oneself, the world, and the future, combined with guilt, despair, insomnia and a general sense of physical discomfort. Both psychotic and neurotic depression are often associated with special types of stress, such as a bereavement or other form of loss. In experiments with dogs, and with people, a state very similar to depression has been induced. The subjects of the experiments were made to feel helpless and this may have triggered the biochemical changes that underlie depression. Recent evidence indicates that experiences early in life and the absence of confiding adult relationships make people vulnerable to depression.

Excessive fear and avoidance of objects or situations are characteristics of anxiety neuroses, which result in the over-arousal of the sympathetic division of the autonomic nervous system, causing heart palpitations, sweating and shakiness, often with irrational thoughts of disaster. The origins of anxiety neurosis are unclear, but many may be caused by frightening experiences.

A phobia is a neurosis in which overwhelming and unreasonable dread of an object or situation severely

The drawing above recreates an experiment that induced depression in dogs. At first only the right side of the enclosed yard was electrified and dogs could escape the mild shock by jumping the barrier. When the left side was electrified and the dogs could not escape even briefly, they gradually became dejected and no longer tried to jump.

disrupts someone's life. One of the commonest phobias is agoraphobia, a fear of going out. Spiders, snakes, mice, thunderstorms, flying, examinations and public speaking can all be objects of phobia.

Obsessive-compulsive disorders are rare neuroses. A patient may be terrified of dirt and invent complicated cleansing rituals that he goes through over and over again, or he may be afraid of burglary and repeatedly undertake elaborate locking routines. In severe cases, the patient's whole time is consumed in these procedures.

Hysteria, from which more women than men suffer, is one of the rarest neuroses, and has two forms, conversion and dissociative. In conversion hysteria parts of the body malfunction without physiological cause, often with partial paralysis or loss of sensation. In dissociative hysteria, aspects of the personality seem to split off, and patients may go into a trance-like state, forgetting everything about themselves.

Two other neuroses, anorexia and bulimia, were once rare but are becoming more common, especially among adolescent girls and young women. Anorexia is an unwillingness to eat, and patients can starve themselves to death. Bulimia is binge eating followed by self-induced vomiting. These life-threatening disorders are difficult to treat if they become severe.

The existence and possible origins of obsessive-compulsive disorder seem to have been understood for centuries. The drawing below of a scene from Shakespeare's play *Macbeth* depicts Lady Macbeth washing her hands because she has become obsessed with the idea that the blood of the king, whom she murdered, remained on her hands long after she had washed them physically clean. Shakespeare was indicating that the crime remained on her conscience and washing away the evidence was insufficient to dispel her anxiety.

The paintings above and below were done by a patient while in the hospital for treatment of severe neurosis. The one above, painted during the height of his disturbance, shows an obsessional attention to detail. In the one below, painted when the patient was much recovered, the overcrowdedness of the first painting is replaced by the openness of the country scene, and has a much less oppressive air.

Medical Treatments

The treatment of mental disturbance has progressed from the primitive idea that insane people were possessed by evil spirits to a compassionate appreciation of the biological and psychological factors that cause so much anguish. Until the early nineteenth century the mentally ill were usually isolated, often in squalor, dark and cold. They were kept on starvation diets, and were subjected to purges and kept in chains, as if deserving punishment not care. When a French physician, Philippe Pinel, removed the chains from his patients in 1793, he not only freed them, but also began the liberation of his profession from its own cruelty and fear.

Since the 1950s a second revolution in the care of the mentally distressed has occurred and the number of patients in mental hospitals has been greatly reduced. This has come about for two reasons – new drugs have become available, and doctors have come to realize that the monotony of a long period in hospital may make patients deteriorate rather than improve. Severe episodes of schizophrenia, manic depression or neuroses may necessitate hospital care at least for a time. Within hospitals, treatment is active, self-help is emphasized, and short stays are encouraged. Success in treating functional psychoses is due mainly to the discovery of the major tranquilizers, the neuroleptics. Schizophrenia responds to them because they block the neurotransmitter dopamine in the limbic system and the prefrontal cortex. These powerful drugs have serious side effects, similar to the symptoms of Parkinson's disease, and can cause problems with movement and muscular coordination. The side effects can be controlled by giving other drugs with the neuroleptics and monitoring the dosage carefully so only the benefits remain. Even if the recovery of a schizophrenic is only partial, with properly balanced medication he can return to ordinary life, to his family or a special hostel.

The hospital storeroom on the right shows a huge number of drugs available to treat not only physical but also mental disorders whether their causes are organic or psychological. There has been a tremendous increase in the number of psychoactive drugs since World War II.

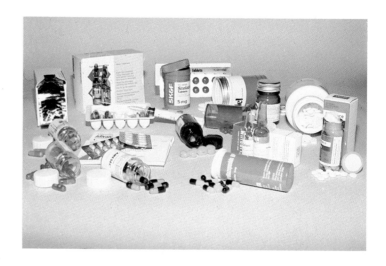

Shown above are samples of drugs mentioned in the text. They come in tablets, capsules, and liquids. Some packaging, such as the strip containing red tablets at the rear, is dated to remind the patient when to take the medication. The ampules on the left are for long acting injections for schizophrenia.

He may then visit a hospital or a local health center only once a month or so for long-acting injections of his medication.

Bipolar manic-depressives can be treated with the salts of the metal lithium, which affect the way chemicals, especially neurotransmitters, cross cell membranes. The drug flattens the highs and lows of the cycle, and patients become outwardly more normal and have less risk of suicide. People who have spells of psychotic depression but no hypomania are often helped by drugs known as tricyclic antidepressants. Some have minor side effects, but they are not addictive and can be gradually withdrawn without causing a relapse. These antidepressants are thought to act by increasing the activity of the neurotransmitter norepinephrine in the brain. Other antidepressants, the Monoamine Oxidase Inhibitors (MAOs), inhibit the breakdown of the same neurotransmitters, thus increasing their amount within the central nervous system. MAOs are usually less effective than the other antidepressants but are more helpful for some patients. Their side effects are mild, but someone taking them must keep to a special diet, avoiding certain foods, especially cheese.

The main drugs used to reduce anxiety in neurotic patients are sedatives to help them sleep, and tranquilizers to help them remain calm. Barbiturates were, until recently, extensively used for both purposes, but

The photograph above shows a room in Bethlem's adolescent unit today. The environment has changed and recovery is now possible.

they are highly addictive. They have been replaced by the benzodiazepines, an example of which is the tranquilizer, Valium. These drugs are much less addictive and safer since it is virtually impossible to take an overdose. However, because they can produce some dependence with prolonged use, doctors agree that these drugs should be used to help someone through a crisis rather than to provide permanent relief.

ECT and Surgery

Apart from drugs, the chief physical methods of treatment for mental illness are electroconvulsive therapy (ECT) and psychosurgery. In ECT, a brief series of electrical shocks is given to the brain by electrodes placed on the skull. Because ECT used to be given without an anaesthetic and it produced muscular convulsions, it was much dreaded by patients and often resisted by relatives. Today it is given under anaesthetic and with a muscle relaxant drug to prevent major convulsions. It is a painless and comparatively safe form of treatment. A course of ECT usually consists of about eight sessions spaced over two or three weeks. Sometimes people are admitted to hospitals for ECT, although it is often given to outpatients.

Although ECT has been used for many different mental disorders from schizophrenia to alcoholism, the evidence suggests that it is beneficial only for severely depressed patients. Patients who already have signs of confusion and memory loss, such as those suffering from senile dementia, should never be given ECT. Like the antidepressant drugs, ECT increases the level of norepinephrine in the brain, and it may be this increased neurotransmitter activity that eases depression. ECT does not work with everyone, but its effects in restoring the depressed patient to a more normal mood can be very dramatic. Some patients who suffer from recurrent depressions must be discouraged by their doctors from demanding ECT every time they feel slightly depressed. Like any other shock to the brain, ECT produces a loss of memory for the events immediately preceding it and it causes patients to feel slightly confused for some hours after the treatment. It causes little, if any, long term impairment to the memory or mental functions, and is nowadays usually administered only to one side of the brain, further reducing side effects.

The other physical method of treatment, a form of brain operation called psychosurgery, was introduced in 1935 and was used a great deal for several years, especially after World War II. Psychosurgery is now rarely used at all except in a few institutions that specialize in the techniques. In the standard operation, known as lobotomy or leucotomy, the nerve fibers connecting the prefrontal cortex to the limbic system are severed. Today smaller and more localized operations are performed, sometimes using minute radioactive implants to destroy specific brain areas. There is little evidence to suggest that this form of psychosurgery

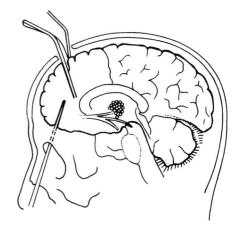
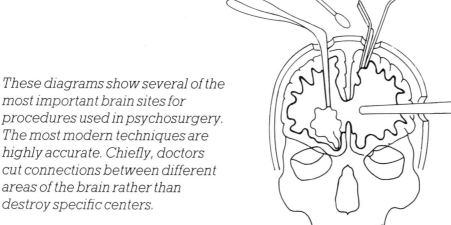

These diagrams show several of the most important brain sites for procedures used in psychosurgery. The most modern techniques are highly accurate. Chiefly, doctors cut connections between different areas of the brain rather than destroy specific centers.

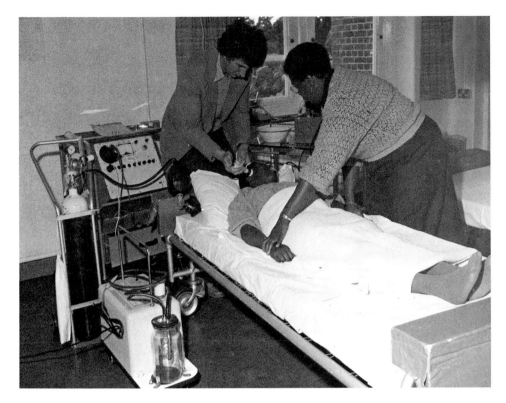

The engraving below, made in 1634, shows trepanation of the head, an ancient technique that dates back before the first century AD and involved drilling holes through the skull. Ancient skulls show evidence of multiple trepanning, which indicates patients survived and sometimes were operated on again.

A patient receiving ECT, as shown above, has no conscious experience during the treatment. The nurse lightly holds the patient's arms to reduce the risk of physical injury from movements induced by the shock. The equipment shown includes a resuscitation unit.

helps mental patients, except possibly those suffering from very severe depression, and even here the evidence is not convincing. The operation usually has very serious side effects, producing apathy and lack of emotion or commitment. The patient is unable to concentrate or to make and execute plans. Because the nerves severed led to the limbic system, which plays a major role in the control of emotion, these side effects are not surprising.

A recent development in psychosurgery is the attempt to cure violently aggressive patients by surgically destroying parts of the amygdala, a component of the limbic system. Removal of the amygdala makes animals extremely tame and lacking in aggression. Since the effects of psychosurgery are irreversible – and the side effects often very serious – it probably should not be used until we have a better understanding of the nerve pathways in the brain controlling emotion.

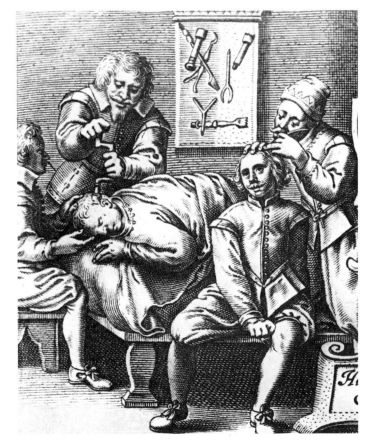

The Unconscious Mind

We are unaware of most of the processes that determine our conscious awareness. Although a person notices when he is thirsty, he is not aware of the underlying physiological mechanisms that create thirst. There are other processes underlying consciousness as well. The preconscious consists of all those memories that one can recall, including those that underlie the "the-tip-of-the-tongue" phenomenon, in which someone senses a memory to be just on the edge of recall. Many unconscious processes, however, can only be brought into conscious awareness if special techniques, such as dream analysis, are used. The unconscious is not a thing or a place, but a name given to a complex set of mental processes that have an indirect but powerful effect on our motives and our emotions.

The idea of the unconscious was first thoroughly investigated by Sigmund Freud (1856-1939), a Viennese doctor who, after studying neurophysiology, concentrated on the origins and treatment of mental illness. His ideas have affected the way people discuss their feelings in everyday life. He was the first psychologist to point out that much of behavior and many emotions are influenced by unconscious wishes. He also believed that all neuroses were caused by unconscious wishes that could not be brought into awareness because the person is ashamed of them.

Freud's conception of the mind can be compared to an iceberg: the small visible tip represents consciousness, and the large underwater bulk, the unconscious. The latter contains the wishes and memories of which people are ashamed. These are said to be repressed, but they still influence conscious thought and behavior. Freud invented psychoanalysis as a means of gaining access to the world of the unconscious. He believed that with this technique, in which an analyst and patient work together to uncover and resolve the unconscious roots of a problem, he could discover the contents of the unconscious. He believed that repressed wishes buried in the unconscious still need to be fulfilled. Since they cannot appear in consciousness, they have to be fulfilled in a disguised way. He called the mental devices that allow such unconscious wish fulfillment defense mechanisms. They defend the person from recognizing the wish for what it is. Slips of the tongue, for example, may indicate a hidden feeling very different from the one that a person intended to express. The phrase "Freudian slip" is now widely used.

Another gateway into the unconscious is through dream analysis. Since the conscious mind is switched

Sigmund Freud, on the right, first used free association as an alternative to hypnosis in 1897. In his lifetime Freud not only created psychoanalysis but a developmental theory of personality as well.

Carl Gustav Jung, on the far right, a Swiss psychologist and psychoanalyst, founded his own school of analytic psychology. Jung emphasized the role of the collective unconscious and the will to live as man's driving force.

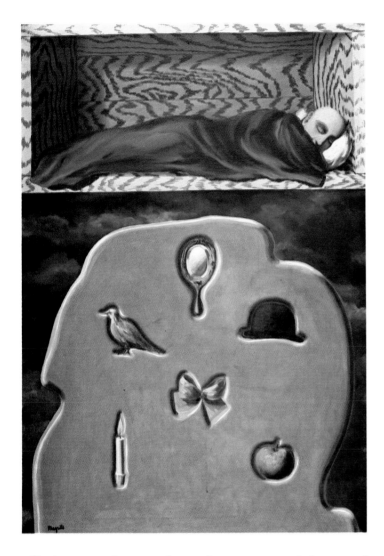

Carl Jung (1875-1961), unhappy with Freud's interpretation of the unconscious, developed his own theories. Jung believed that the individual unconscious arises from an inborn, collective unconscious. This view profoundly influenced the sort of analysis that Jung, and later his pupils, came to practice. Dreams are the voice of the collective unconscious and their symbols are the "archetypes," that is, basic ideas like Earth Mother, Wise Old Man, Animus (masculinity), Anima (femininity). Jung found that these basic archetypes in his patients' dreams were often represented as different aspects of the patient's personality, such as the masculine or feminine sides, good or evil, part or whole. In dreams, even an everyday scene could take the form of a message from one or more archetypes. Jung believed that if a patient gained access to his archetypes, he would be able to grow and fulfil himself.

Although it is now widely accepted that unconscious processes exist, there is considerable debate about their role in the cause of psychological disturbance. Psychoanalysts who came after Freud have changed his theories to take more account of conscious experience and the importance of social relationships. The intellectual tradition that Freud began has flourished for nearly one hundred years, although it has received little support from the attempts made to test it objectively.

off when people are asleep, the content and themes of dreams are signs of the unconscious mind at work. The surface content of the dream, according to Freud, often disguises unconscious wishes in symbols. Freud thought the true significance of the dream could be discovered by interpreting it in the light of the associations the dreamer gives to the events in it. The dream may reflect a present conflict between the dreamer's unconscious and conscious wishes, or it may be a symbolic representation of events in the distant past. The symbols that appear can show the roots of a current problem. When the unconscious mind affects the conscious, the links between persons, situations and emotions are made in oblique or symbolic ways in order to disguise the unconscious wishes.

Freud's work brought the concept of the unconscious mind fully into Western culture. One of his students,

Psychoanalysis

Psychoanalysis is a set of techniques devised by Freud to investigate and treat mental disturbance. The techniques include free association of thoughts by the patient, the analysis of dreams and slips of the tongue, and the analysis of the patient's reaction to the analyst, known as transference, since according to Freud the patient treats his analyst in the same way he treated his parents. Although there are various types of analysis, the form is similar in each school. A single session usually lasts fifty minutes. In full analysis, the patient returns three to five times a week, to the same place, at the same time each day for a period of between three to five years. Throughout the analysis, the responsibility to speak is the patient's. Orthodox Freudian analysts offer few interpretations and little support. They believe it is important for the patient to discover his own psyche himself.

In Freudian analysis the therapist makes sense of the patient's distress by using three main aspects of theory – the development of personality, defense mechanisms, and the relationship between ego, id and superego. Freud's developmental theory holds that the "libido," or basic driving force, is focused successively on different parts of the body. The oral stage, which lasts for the first year of life, centers on the mouth. The second year is the anal stage, in which during toilet training the child gains satisfaction from the conflicting pleasures of eliminating and holding on. From about three to five years of age, the phallic stage develops, and children begin to derive pleasure from stimulating their genitals. They observe the differences between male and female and unconsciously direct their emerging sexual desire towards the parent of the opposite sex. The Oedipus complex is the name given to the sexual desire of a young boy for his mother and Electra complex to the young girl's desire for her father. The latent stage follows, in which the libido is dormant and pleasure is gained from manipulating and learning to control the environment. At puberty, the genital stage emerges, and the young person begins to express adult sexual feeling.

Freud believed that each of these stages brought with them its own conflicts. If at one stage, the child fails

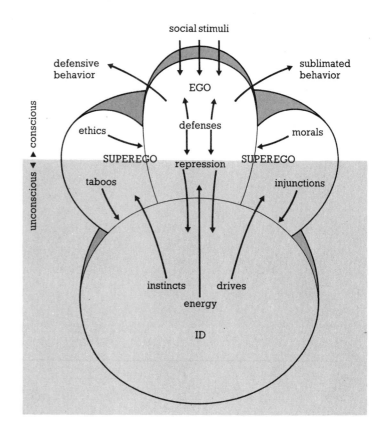

This diagram shows the relationships between the id, the ego and the superego. The id is unconscious, the ego is largely conscious and the superego is mostly unconscious. The ego referees between the basic desires of the id and the social and moral restraints imposed by the superego. Thus it generates forms of behavior that are socially acceptable and satisfy, at least in part, the id.

to reconcile his own wishes with the demands of his parents, part of his personality may remain unconsciously locked in conflict.

The analyst pays attention to the ways the client disguises unconscious wishes. These disguises result from the use of defense mechanisms, such as sublimation and projection. In anal fixation, for example, the original conflict may be converted by sublimation into the hoarding of money. By projection, a stingy person may hide this trait from himself by repeatedly accusing

The engraving right, made in 1910, is an early cartoon showing Freud analyzing himself. Out of the figure on the couch rise symbols of a Freudian dream: a small figure gesturing to a door that opens on nothing is trapped inside Freud's own giant head.

others of being stingy. There are many such mechanisms, but all are designed to keep unacceptable wishes out of consciousness.

To link defense mechanisms with personality structure and show the relationship between the conscious and unconscious, Freud proposed the tripartite theory of mind: id, ego and superego. The id is unconscious and contains all the repressed wishes. The ego is the conscious part of the mind, which perceives, remembers and feels. The superego develops in people as they take into themselves aspects of their parents' moral code. It operates as a censor and governs the way in which material in the id will appear in the conscious ego.

With all this in mind, the analyst tries to uncover repressed wishes, so that the original feelings associated with an unresolved conflict may be relived and more successfully resolved. Psychoanalysts believe that the patient is then freed from his defensive behavior and can sublimate the original thwarted wishes in a more healthy way.

In traditional forms of psychoanalysis, such as is shown left, the patient lies on a couch with the analyst sitting to one side or behind.

Psychotherapy

Psychotherapy is the attempt to alleviate mental distress through the patient or client talking to a trained psychotherapist. There are today many different schools of psychotherapy. Most place less emphasis on recovering childhood conflicts than did Freud, but some still use some of the ideas of psychoanalysis, including the existence of unconscious wishes. Modern psychotherapists tend to examine the client's present conflicts and relationships. The psychotherapist tries to develop a trusting and confiding relationship with the client, within which he may try, for example, to help the client see that he is feeling too much guilt or that he is unnecessarily dependent on someone else. Many modern psychotherapists emphasize personal growth and self-fulfillment.

One of the leaders of the modern psychotherapy movement was an American, Carl Rogers. He developed a form of psychotherapy known as client-centered or non-directive therapy. He never gave the patient direct advice or made any interpretations of what the client said. Instead, he encouraged clients to talk freely to him, prompted them by asking questions and then merely reflected their own words back to them. He believed that to be successful, a therapist had to exhibit three qualities – genuineness, warmth

Art therapy uses painting and sculpture as vehicles for emotional expression. Much of what might be obscured, especially by less verbal or handicapped patients, may be revealed by self-expression in these ways. This setting also allows a good relationship to develop between therapist and patient.

A dance therapy group shown right helps mental patients to use full physical movement and cope with ordinary social situations.

toward the client and empathy. Rogers believed that provided the patient talked openly, and provided the therapist exhibited these qualities, the client would himself come to sort out his own emotional problems.

Another well-known movement is Gestalt therapy, founded by Frederic Perls. Perls believed that the neurotic plays games or false roles, and the therapist's task is to enable him to see his true self. In attempting to strip off the false layers that hide the true self Gestalt therapists sometimes act in highly aggressive ways toward their clients. They may also try to make the client concentrate on the immediate present, and avoid thinking about the past or the future.

Much psychotherapy is conducted in groups. A married couple, for example, are usually asked to attend sessions together. Ideally, both a male and female therapist are present so that neither individual feels that the therapist and spouse are in alliance against him or her. By observing how couples interact, the therapists may be able to point out patterns of irrational or incompatible behavior that lead to strife. Family therapy is an extension of marital therapy.

In the most common form of group therapy eight or

In a typical bioenergetic analysis workshop, the therapist is working with a client stretched over a breathing stool. This simple apparatus has several uses and helps correct breathing. Such exercises and the interpretations of the therapist help a person understand and resolve inner conflicts through seeing them physically expressed.

ten strangers meet for an hour or two once or twice a week. In theory, group therapy has many advantages. First, it saves the therapist's time and is therefore less expensive. Second, it helps the patient see that his troubles are not unique. Third, if the group is supportive, patients can learn to express distressing feelings and find that being honest does not lead to rejection. Finally, any difficulties the patient has in social interactions become obvious in a group and can be pointed out in a supportive and caring way. Thus patients can come to see themselves and others more objectively.

Encounter groups, which are designed to increase people's sensitivity to themselves and others, are not intended for severely neurotic patients. Some neurotic people, however, are attracted to them and it can be dangerous if groups are not run by skilled therapists.

There are much less conventional forms of therapy, such as "primal scream," in which patients are encouraged to scream and let out basic psychic pain, and bioenergetics, in which patients recognize their conflicts through body posture and the interpretations of the therapist. Few tests have been made of the efficacy of such treatment, and even the evidence for the effectiveness of psychotherapy in general is mixed.

Above is shown a family and their therapist. Group treatments recently have begun to use ideas related specifically to group psychgology, and other ideas from biology and electronics, especially communications and systems theory, are now being brought into psychological treatment.

Behavior Therapy

Since the 1960s, behavior therapy has been developed by psychologists and doctors as an alternative to traditional psychotherapy. At first behavioral treatment was based solely on learning theory. Now, more realistically, it is loosely based on the more general principles of experimental psychology. Behavior therapists believe that neurotic symptoms arise from inappropriate learning experiences. Behavior therapists attempt to teach patients methods of changing their behavior, believing that feelings depend on behavior and that if someone behaves appropriately, he will also come to have the appropriate emotions.

Initial success was achieved in the treatment of phobias, using techniques similar to Pavlovian extinction. Behavior therapy has been extended to the training of the mentally handicapped and many neurotic and psychotic disorders. In the treatment of phobias, systematic "counter-conditioning" techniques have been used extensively. For example, a patient afraid of spiders may be taught to relax fully, then asked to place in order the least to the most terrifying situations involving spiders. Seeing a small spider at a distance may be the least frightening, and a large hairy tarantula crawling up one's leg might be the most. The patient is then again asked to relax and form a mental image of the least frightening situation. If relaxation is disturbed by fear, the patient is immediately instructed to go back in imagination to a less terrifying situation. The idea is that relaxation is incompatible with fear. The patient becomes conditioned to relax to thoughts of spiders and hence to the actual sight of spiders. Another method, known as flooding, makes use of extinction. The patient is exposed directly to the object of fear and is kept in the situation until the fear subsides completely.

Weight Watchers was the first organization to use a group behavioral treatment for obesity. A constructive approach and the individual tailoring of goals, combined with the supportive structure of a friendly group, are used to build new eating behavior patterns necessary to control weight permanently.

In the belief that behavior occurs because it is reinforced, therapists may treat a severely overactive child, for example, by first watching how the people around the child reinforce it. Because the child attracts attention by being active but is ignored when quiet, the therapist attempts to reverse the reinforcement conditions. Overactive behavior receives less attention while quiet behavior receives full attention and praise until the child learns to discriminate the new pattern of reinforcement. Behavior therapy is also widely used in the treatment of addictions and obesity. The patient is encouraged to practice the new behavior outside the therapist's office and to report back the results at the next session.

In general, behavior therapy makes great use of

The autistic children left are being reinforced by attention and praise for constructive and cooperative activity. Although the teacher pays attention to the activity she is reinforcing, she must also be aware of the uninvolved child so that any subsequent attempt to join in may be reinforced when it occurs.

The autistic children above are guided through a new behavior pattern and then immediately rewarded by praise and attention. In a complex series of actions, each step is guided and reinforced. The chain of actions is then gradually put together. This technique is used in behavior modification with children and the mentally handicapped.

rewards for appropriate behavior. The reward may often be nothing more than praise. It appears to be important to suggest that the patient reward himself, by self-congratulation, perhaps, or by a treat. In severely disturbed hospital patients, rewards are often used to counteract apathy. A "token economy" regime may be set up under which the patient receives tokens for appropriate behavior. The tokens can be exchanged for various rewards, such as candy, cigarettes or watching television. The sort of behavior that earns tokens might include being clean and tidy, eating properly with a knife and fork, or helping clear the table after meals.

The techniques of behavior therapy are often used on one problem at a time. At the beginning of therapy, a list of problem behaviors may be drawn up in the form of a contract that also sets out the goals of treatment. The responsibility for change rests with the patient. The therapist tries to teach the patient to alter or over-come problem behavior by providing both active techniques and support. Which techniques the therapist uses are tailored to the special nature of the patient's problems. In practice, most behavior thera-pists do not use purely behavioral methods. They also try to help patients develop insight into their behavior and teach them to think more clearly and rationally about themselves.

Hypnosis

Hypnosis is a technique for inducing a trance-like state in which the behavior and feelings of the person hypnotized can be strongly influenced by suggestions made by the hypnotist. Hypnosis is one of the strangest forms of psychological phenomena, but careful research has shown that it is difficult to fake. Although people who are asked to pretend to be hypnotized can mimic some of the effects of hypnosis, they cannot fake them completely.

Hypnosis produces changes in conscious awareness. It resembles the sort of trance experienced in dissociative hysteria, during which the patient may lose consciousness of certain aspects of reality. Under hypnosis, some part of the mind becomes separated from the rest and this part obeys the hypnotist's instructions. Although the subject may appear to be asleep, the brain waves are those of someone who is alert and awake.

The usual method of inducing a hypnotic trance is to suggest to the subject that he is feeling drowsy and to get him to relax more and more deeply, perhaps by presenting a monotonous repetitive stimulus, such as a watch swinging back and forth on a chain. The hypnotist then gently makes suggestions, perhaps saying that the subject's eyes are closing and he will find himself breathing more and more heavily. Since this is usually true, it enhances the hypnotist's control. He then may test the strength of the trance by telling the subject he can no longer say the word "five" and ask him to count to ten. If the hypnosis is working, the subject will omit the number five although he may later report that he felt he could have said it if he had tried hard enough. As the level of hypnosis deepens, stronger and stronger suggestions can be made to the

In the consulting room of Franz Mesmer, right, clients sitting around a tank are supposed to intensify their magnetic force when they grasp the rods. This was the setting for many cures using hypnotism or "mesmerism." In 1784 a French Royal Commission declared Mesmer's work worthless. Investigations continued and hypnotism is now known to have valid therapeutic effects.

subject, some of which he may act upon only after coming out of the trance. The hypnotist may say, for example, that when he blows his nose the subject must open an umbrella in the room. Later the subject obeys this instruction without remembering he had received it. When asked why he opened the umbrella he makes up an explanation to make his own behavior appear sensible, if only to satisfy himself.

It is sometimes said that only rather weak-willed people can be hypnotized, but this is almost the reverse of the truth. The best hypnotic subjects are those who are capable of going into a state of total absorption in their normal lives. About twenty per cent of the population can enter a deep trance. When told they will not feel pain, they will allow the hypnotist to stick pins in their fingers without protest. Whether people

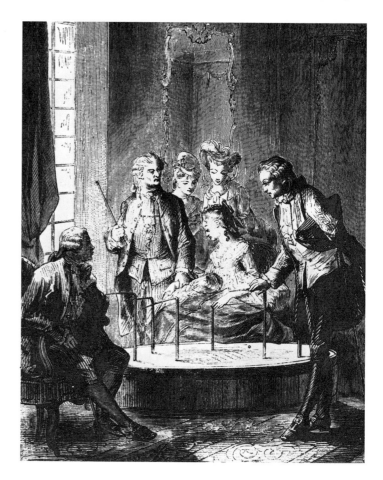

In the photograph below an appendectomy is taking place under hypnosis. The patient is able to talk to doctors throughout the thirty-minute operation and feels no pain.

In 1881 Jean Charcot, above, used hynosis as a means to study the physical and neurological effects of hysterical reactions in his patients. Sigmund Freud traveled to Paris to study with him, saw demonstrations like this, and later used hypnosis in the early stages of his development of psychoanalysis. Freud's technique allowed patients to relive past experiences that troubled their minds.

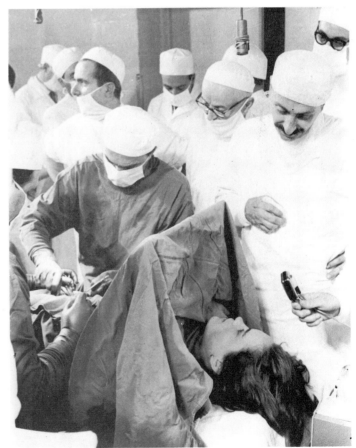

can be hypnotized against their will is much debated.

Hypnosis can be used to help some people. For example, it is now quite widely used to help people to bear pain more readily. Hypnosis can have an effect, although sometimes only a temporary one, on dieting and giving up smoking. Self-hypnosis techniques are also being tried for psychosomatic disorders, such as asthma and eczema. One of the oddest and best demonstrated uses of hypnosis is for curing warts. In one experiment, people suffering from warts were told under hypnosis that the warts would disappear from the left side of their bodies. In most subjects the warts did disappear from the left side. The warts on the right side remained, and in later hypnotic sessions the people were told that those too would disappear – and they did.

Brainwashing and Mind Control

Brainwashing is a term that was coined during the Korean War to describe attempts made by Chinese interrogators brought in by the North Koreans to try to convert American prisoners of war to communism. Starvation, sleep deprivation, torture and drugs were used to weaken the prisoners. They were kept in isolation so that they could not be supported in their beliefs by their comrades, and systematic attempts were made to reduce their confidence and self-esteem through ridicule and humiliation. A prisoner would be kept for long periods in a dark, soundless cell with no furniture, a technique known as sensory deprivation, which tends to produce feelings of disorientation and a loss of personal identity. A team of brutal interrogators often alternated with a team that was kind and tried to persuade the prisoner that it was in his best interest to change his views or confess to some alleged crime. The contrast between the brutality of one and the kind-ness of the other may have encouraged the prisoners to develop trust in one group at a time when their determination to resist was lowered by physical weakness, loss of pride and mental confusion.

Some of the techniques, such as sensory deprivation, were partly derived from the discoveries of psychological research. Others were not new but have been used by torturers throughout the centuries and are well documented in history. Under prolonged treatment, only someone of quite exceptional strength will refuse to confess to some crime, imaginary or real, or sign documents on demand. It is extremely rare, however, for even prolonged brainwashing to change a person's ideas and beliefs. Despite attempts to convert them to communism, fewer than fifty of the 4500 American prisoners decided to stay in Korea at the end of the war. In 1957 the Hungarian Communist government was able to extract a confession in open court from

Jozsef Cardinal Mindszenty of Hungary is shown here before (right) and after (far right) interrogation during which many psychological techniques were used to extract his confession to crimes against the State. The world was shocked by the dramatic change in his appearance.

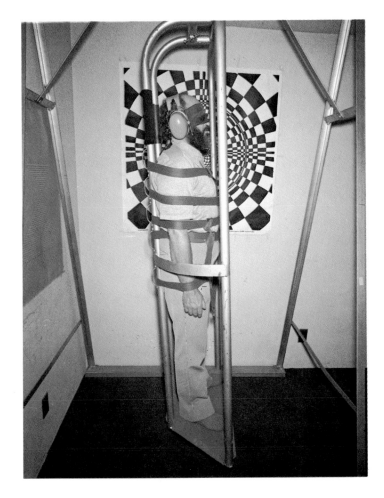

Sensory deprivation can be induced by equipment shown in the photograph at left being used at a medical center in Brooklyn. Scientists have made an environment similar to a "witches' cradle," which was once used to cause trance-like states for medieval witches. Modern apparatus is used to study the effects on volunteers isolated from normal sensory data from a few hours to two days.

The film 1984, *taken from the novel of the same name by George Orwell, is about a man, played by Edmond O'Brien, who tenaciously resists succumbing to mind control.*

Cardinal Mindszenty, but, as his autobiography later demonstrated, they failed to convert him.

B.F. Skinner believes that even without brainwashing people's beliefs and actions can be shaped, if the rewards and punishments they receive from birth onwards are absolutely controlled. For several reasons, this idea is almost certainly wrong. First, it is possible to reward people only for what they do, not for what they think. Second, complete control over rewards and punishments can be achieved only inside a totally self-contained environment, which is a practical impossibility. Third, some rewards are purely internal; a person may maintain his own beliefs out of a sense of pride or inner standards, and his success in continuing to hold his beliefs despite great efforts to change them may be rewarding in itself.

It has been suggested that in the future advancing knowledge of the brain might enable people to control others by direct interference with the brain itself. Although brain operations can alter mood, they also damage people's performance in ordinary life. No operation could systematically change someone's beliefs or goals and leave the rest of his abilities and potential untouched. It is possible to change brain function by electrical stimulation, but a single stimulation affects many different systems within the brain and the results are unpredictable. They vary not only from one person to another but also within a single individual. It will probably never be possible to control beliefs completely by psychological means or by direct interference with such a finely adjusted system as the brain.

Mind in the Future

Many different sciences contribute to our knowledge of the human mind, including psychology, neurophysiology, neuroanatomy, neurochemistry, and the branch of computer science that is called artificial intelligence.

It is the computer that is providing the key to many developments in the investigation of the mind. Although no computer program matches the mind's flexibility, we can already design programs that model the steps the mind takes in carrying out particular tasks, such as visual perception or problem solving. In the not too distant future, better programs for understanding speech and producing artificial speech will be written. Such programs have practical aplications – among others, for blind persons, who could use a machine that translates print into artificial speech, or one that "sees" obstacles in the path. Indeed, prototypes of both these machines have already been built.

The computer is the heart of techniques invented in the 1970s to investigate the brain directly. The CAT scan – Computerized Axial Tomography – takes two-dimensional X-ray pictures from a great many points and assembles them by computer to give a three-dimensional look at any part of the body. As a tool to examine the human brain, the CAT scan pinpoints structural damage. But the CAT scan's picture is static. A more recent development, the PETT scan – for Positron-Emission Transaxial Tomography – also uses computer-generated pictures, but to watch the brain at work. Tiny amouts of short-lived radioactive tracers are injected and taken up by the neurons, making it possible to chart the brain's metabolism.

In a third and still developing technique, called NMR, for Nuclear Magnetic Resonance, the computer is used to generate even more accurate pictures. The brain, or another part of the body, is briefly subjected to a magnetic field so that certain atoms align into decipherable patterns. NMR may become useful both for detecting structural problems, like CAT, and studying brain function, like PETT.

In brain chemistry, the computer can be used to make molecular models of the natural substances that block receptor sites for neurotransmitters. Chemists can take this information and try to construct new molecules of the same shape to act as artificial blockers, which will help to regulate faulty neurotransmitter activity. Further work on transmitters such as enkephalins and endorphins could conceivably lead to the discovery of drugs that would relieve pain without dangerous side effects.

Possibly, too, this path leads to new chemical treatments for certain mental disturbances. There has been modest progress in psychotherapy in recent years. Although it is unlikely to become a panacea for neurosis, some further progress is likely to be made. Scientists are learning more about the causes of mental disorder, but it is difficult to persuade people to avoid the stressful lives that cause ill-health.

We can expand our knowledge of the mind, but it is doubtful whether we can ever reach a full understanding of it. The way an individual mind works depends not only on the mechanisms of the brain but on a person's whole experience and knowledge, which are unmeasurable. Original thought and discoveries are made in ways that will probably never be completely understood. We can always look forward to knowing more, but never to understanding all.

The PETT scan equipment shown opposite is relaying through the crown of tubes the impulses produced by specific areas of a woman's brain after she has been injected with radioactive glucose. This apparatus has produced the blood flow pictures used throughout the book.

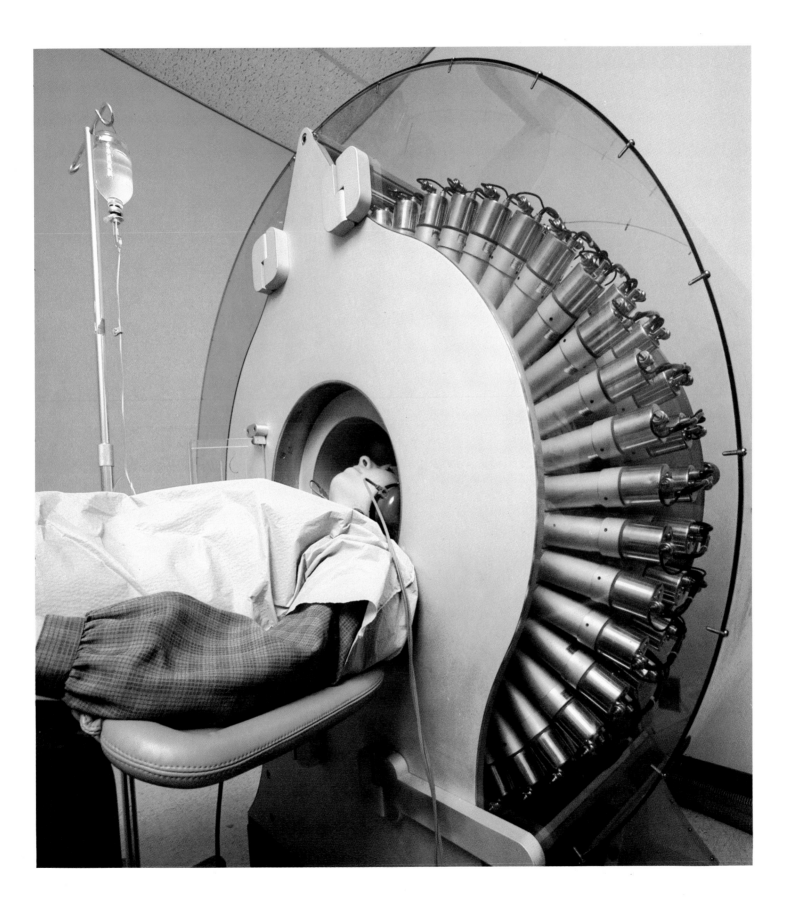

Glossary

Axon: part of a neuron, a long thin fiber by which one neuron contacts other neurons

Cell: the smallest unit of living matter that can function independently. It is enclosed by a membrane and its activities are regulated by a dense body within it, the nucleus.

Central nervous system: the brain and the spinal cord

Conditioning: a learning process, or the result of one, involving changes in behavior

Conscious: being aware of one's surroundings and what one is thinking and feeling

Cortex: the wrinkled outer layer of the brain, which envelops the top and sides of the two halves, and which reaches its highest development in man, and plays a vital role in movement, speech, sight and thought

Creativity: the ability to think and act in an original, imaginative and constructive way

Depression: an emotional state characterized by gloom and a lack of vitality, which when severe, is considered a mental illness

Dopamine: a neurotransmitter in the brain. Imbalance in its activity plays a significant role in both Parkinson's disease and schizophrenia.

Drive: a motive for action. Some drives are for biological needs, such as warmth and food, others are for goals established by society, such as success in work.

ECT: electroconvulsive therapy, popularly known as electric shock treatment, in which patients are given electric shocks to the brain to help ease the symptoms of mental disorder, usually depression

Electrode: a terminal that can direct a mild electric current into a specific area of the brain or body, or can receive the electrical impulses being produced there

Electroencephalogram: a record of the wave-like patterns of electrical activity produced by the brain, and measured by electrodes placed on the scalp. The instrument used to record these is called an encephalograph or an electroencephalograph.

Endorphins/enkephalins: neurotransmitters in the brain that reduce pain by acting in a way very similar to the drug morphine

Genetic: relating to inheritance, and referring to those qualities that are transferred from parents to offspring by genes, minute structures within cells that are passed on by sex cells

Glands: special groups of cells that withdraw certain substances from the blood and put back into it other substances called hormones, which act on the internal chemistry and affect actions and general health

Hypnosis: a method of inducing a state of mind combining the features of sleep with semi-conscious trance, in which a person may accept suggestions very readily

Hypothalamus: a pea-sized structure that coordinates many important activities and emotions, such as hunger, thirst, anxiety and aggression

Illness: a harmful disturbance of one's physical or mental processes. Illnesses may be treated in many ways, from simple rest, diet and counseling to more complicated processes that may involve drugs, surgery or psychotherapy.

Impulse: a sudden change in electrical potential that starts in the cell body of a neuron and travels along its axon; also, a sudden desire to carry out some unplanned action

Libido: according to Freudian theory, the strong life energy, a major aspect of which is the sex drive

Limbic system: a set of structures that regulate many types of behavior, such as excitement, relaxation, eating, sexual activity, emotions and response to rewards

Motor neuron: a neuron that carries impulses from the central nervous system to muscles and glands

Neuron: an individual nerve cell

Neurotransmitter: a chemical substance that carries information from one neuron to another

Neurosis: one of a number of common and less severe forms of mental disorder that involve inappropriate behavior and emotions

Peripheral nervous system: the nerves and nerve cells that carry information between the central nervous system and the rest of the body

Personality: the total intellectual, emotional and physical characteristics that make up the way an individual behaves.

Phobia: a severe and disabling fear of some object or situation

Placebo: a harmless substance with no therapeutic value that is given to a patient who believes it to be medication

Psychiatry: the branch of medicine that deals with mental and emotional illness

Psychiatrist: a doctor with specialist qualifications in psychiatry

Psychology: the systematic study of behavior and the mind

Psychologist: a person with academic and practical or research qualifications in psychology. A clinical psychologist is trained in the diagnosis and treatment of emotional, behavioral and mental disorders. An experimental psychologist is trained to concentrate on laboratory research into psychological principles.

Psychosis: serious mental illness in which the sufferer is out of touch with reality and behavior is very disturbed

Receptor: a neuron that is excited by events outside the nervous system

Reflex: an involuntary response to stimulus. If a response has been learned, it is called a conditioned reflex (or a conditioned response).

Reinforcement; a pleasurable event or reward that makes it more likely that the organism will repeat the behavior that preceded it .

Schizophrenia: one of a number of severe mental disorders, the symptoms of which often include grossly inappropriate emotional responses, hearing and seeing non-existent things, and withdrawal from reality

Sensory neuron: a neuron that carries impulses from any of the receptors to the central nervous system

Sociopathy: a very severe form of personality disorder. A sociopath is very antisocial and often criminal.

Stimulus: any event detected by receptor cells that triggers either physiological or mental processes

Synapse: the junction between two neurons where one affects the other by releasing neurotransmitters. All neurons have many synapses.

Therapy: actions undertaken to cure an illness or relieve distress

Unconscious: a state of mental unawareness, and the different processes of the mind that influence memories, motives and emotions

Index

Credits

The publishers gratefully acknowledge permission to reproduce the following illustrations:

Ardes 13*r*; Associated Press 90*l*, *r*; Bettman Archive 79*b*, 83*t*; Biophoto Associates 13*c*; P. Brierley 22; Camera Press 53*c*; Lean-Loup Charmet 89*t*; Edward de Bono © the Cognitive Research Trust Ltd. 1972 63*b*; Colorific! 38*l*, 43*r*, 71*t*, 91*t*; Daily Telegraph Colour Library 81, 65; Mary Evans 9, 77*t*, 80*l*,*r*; Fotomas Index 63*t*; Henry Grant 42; Guttman Maclay Collection 75*t*, *bl*; James Hands 87*t*; John Hillelsen Agency 11*t*, *b*, 41*b*, 51*b*, 71*b*, 84*b*; H. Huber, Bern Verlag 54*t*; Alan Hutchison 55*l*, *r*, 66*l*, *r*; Image Bank 61; Institute of Dermatology 45*l*; Keystone Press 89*b*; N. Lassen 3, 19, 23, 25*l*, 27*t*; J. Laure courtesy Lewis Lippsitt 48*t*; Nat Farbman/Life Magazine © Time Inc. 33*b*; Max Waldman/Life Magazine © Time Inc 72*b*; Mander & Mitchenson 75*br*; L. von Matt 24; National Film Archive 91*b*; National Museum Vincent van Gogh 73; For the National Society for Autistic Children by Camilla Jessel 87*b*; M. Abrahams/Network 77*b*; Novosti 48*b*; J. Olds 17; G. Patmore 49*l*; Photo Researchers Inc. 54*b*; Picturepoint 49*r*, 72*t*; Pixfeatures 53*b*; Post & Times Newspaper, Leek, Staffs 86; Dan McCoy, Rainbow 93; Rex Features 38*r*; Ann Ronan 88; Science Photo Library 37; M. Slatford 46; Tony Stone Associates 52*l*; D. Reed/Sunday Times 59; By courtesy of Prof. N.S. Sutherland, Lab. of Experimental Psychology, University of Sussex 51*t*; Tate Gallery 81; John Topham 52*r*, 53*t*; U.P.I. photo 15, 69; Vision International 27*b*, 43*l*, 56, 67, 76*b*, 83*b*, 85*b*; J. Watney 6, 13*l*, 28, 84*t*; WB Pharmaceuticals Ltd. 45*b*; By courtesy of the Wellcome Trustees 41*t*; Geoffrey Whitfield, Brighton 85*t*.

Artwork by: Richard Gliddon 24, 82; Tom McArthur 7, 8, 13, 14, 16, 18, 19, 20, 21, 22, 26, 28, 29, 30, 34, 35, 36, 39, 40, 44, 47, 50, 57, 60, 64, 65, 68, 70, 78; Carol McCleeve 10, 15, 17, 23, 32, 37, 43, 46, 56, 58, 59, 69; Jerro Roy 62, 74.

Cover photograph: Michael Freeman

Bibliography

Breakdown, N. S. Sutherland, New American Library, 1977
Eye and Brain, R. L. Gregory, McGraw Hill, 1966
Introduction to Psychology, E. R. Hilgard, et al, Harcout Brace Jovanovich, 1979
Psychology & Medicine: Psychobiological Dimensions of Health and Illness, Donald A. Bakal, Springer Publishing Co., 1979
Psychology: The Science of Mental Life, George A. Miller & Robert Buckhout, Harper & Row, 1973
Psychology Today: An Introduction, (4th edn), Communications Research Machines Inc., Random House, 1979